MW01274436

Martin Kramer, *University of California, Berkeley*
EDITOR-IN-CHIEF

Important Lessons from Innovative Colleges and Universities

V. Ray Cardozier
University of Texas, Austin

EDITOR

Number 82, Summer 1993

JOSSEY-BASS PUBLISHERS
San Francisco

IMPORTANT LESSONS FROM INNOVATIVE COLLEGES AND UNIVERSITIES
V. Ray Cardozier (ed.)
New Directions for Higher Education, no. 82
Martin Kramer, Editor-in-Chief

Microfilm copies of issues and articles are available in 16mm and 35mm, as well as microfiche in 105mm, through University Microfilms Inc., 300 North Zeeb Road, Ann Arbor, Michigan 48106.

LC 85-644752   ISSN 0271-0560   ISBN 1-55542-690-5

NEW DIRECTIONS FOR HIGHER EDUCATION is part of The Jossey-Bass Higher and Adult Education Series and is published quarterly by Jossey-Bass Inc., Publishers, 350 Sansome Street, San Francisco, California 94104-1310 (publication number USPS 990-880). Second-class postage paid at San Francisco, California, and at additional mailing offices. POSTMASTER: Send address changes to New Directions for Higher Education, Jossey-Bass Inc., Publishers, 350 Sansome Street, San Francisco, California 94104-1310.

SUBSCRIPTIONS for 1993 cost $45.00 for individuals and $60.00 for institutions, agencies, and libraries.

EDITORIAL CORRESPONDENCE should be sent to the Editor-in-Chief, Martin Kramer, 2807 Shasta Road, Berkeley, California 94708.

Cover photograph and random dot by Richard Blair/Color & Light © 1990.

The paper used in this journal is acid-free and meets the strictest guidelines in the United States for recycled paper (50 percent recycled waste, including 10 percent postconsumer waste). Manufactured in the United States of America.

Contents

EDITOR'S NOTES

In the decade from 1960 to 1970, college enrollment grew from 3.5 million to 8.5 million, swelled not only by the baby boom that reached campuses during the 1960s but also by changes in societal attitudes about who could and should go to college. The percentage of the eligible age group enrolling in college had been expanding since the end of World War II.

Legislatures converted teachers colleges and junior colleges into state colleges and later into state universities; private colleges were absorbed into state systems; and hundreds of two-year institutions were established to meet the growing demand for college education. In addition, almost one hundred new state-supported baccalaureate-level institutions and hundreds of private colleges and universities were founded to serve the expanding college population.

During this period of expansion, many college administrators and faculty were questioning the traditional objectives, practices, and policies of American higher education. New ideas began to appear in programs of national conferences and in professional journals concerning the organization of institutions and the provision of educational services. Hundreds of long-established institutions experimented with new ways in which to better serve their clientele: facilitation of the admissions process for categories of students not previously served, enhancement and simplification of learning, and provision of curricula that better prepared students for the world of work. But the most extensive experimentation took place in newly created institutions, which were unhampered by tradition and which attracted faculty and administrators who wished to participate in the founding of institutions built around the ideas set forth by the planners. A considerable number of these newly created institutions experimented with a variety of innovations designed not only to improve the education process but also to challenge the basic purposes of higher education.

This volume, *Important Lessons from Innovative Colleges and Universities*, is about seven of those institutions and the innovations that they instituted. (The term *innovation* is used here not in the sense of a unique or completely new practice or policy but rather as a departure from the traditional.) Our objectives are to describe the innovations, to assess how well each worked, and in the cases of those that did not succeed or that did not live up to the planners' expectations, to discuss reasons. Each chapter is, in effect, a case study of an experiment in putting a combination of ideas into practice, utilizing the input of the academic community over a period of time.

The growth and changing geographical distribution of the U.S. population will almost certainly call for the establishment of a number of new institutions in the decade ahead. Some planners will be inspired by the opportunity for innovation from the ground up, as was the case for the colleges and universities examined here. Our hope is that this volume will prove useful not only to individuals charged with planning new colleges but also to those in established institutions who are considering changes in objectives, practices, and policies. In a broader sense, however, these chapters are intended to share with the entire academic community—faculty, administrators, students, trustees, legislators, and others concerned with colleges and universities. While the experience of the institutions described here does not necessarily validate or invalidate ideas for all education settings, it can inform the deliberation process and help planners perform their tasks more effectively. The lessons of this body of experience can also benefit those who innovate on a smaller scale.

All of these institutions are now more than twenty years old. Most of them and their innovations have been discussed previously, at least in part, in the literature. However, this book differs in two important ways. First, some of the previous reports appeared before the institutions opened and focus only on institutional plans. Others appeared shortly after the institutions opened, when the innovations had not yet been tested adequately. All of the institutions discussed in this book have now been in operation long enough for the innovations to be examined at length; in addition, sufficient time has passed to provide perspective on whether the institutions' assessments of their own performance within a decade after opening are valid in retrospect.

Second, most writing about innovative institutions is by authors who were not involved in the planning of the institutions. While this outsider perspective is, in some ways, an advantage in the assessment of outcomes, it does have inherent limitations. Specifically, the author may not fully understand planners' expectations and therefore may not be fully able to assess results. Alternatively, the author may, wittingly or unwittingly, assess the outcomes of innovations in terms of what he or she thinks should have been achieved. This limitation is analogous to that of the book reviewer who reacts to a book not in terms of the author's purpose in writing it but rather according to what he or she thinks the author should have attempted to write, or what the reviewer would have written if he or she had authored the book.

In this volume, the author, or senior author in the case of coauthors, of each chapter was one of the planners of the institution about which he writes. He was personally involved in planning the institution and has personal knowledge of what the planners hoped to achieve with each innovation. The amount of influence or input that each author had in defining the mission of the institution and the innovations that were attempted varies, but in each case the writer is acquainted through personal experience with the original plans.

The authors examine their respective institutions and the innovations over at least the first ten years of operation. Most project their assessments to the present day; three senior authors chose coauthors who are currently administrators in the institutions examined in order to extend their analyses to the present time. Moreover, the authors assess the innovations in terms of their own perceptions of what was envisioned in the original plans, rather than in terms of external criteria. No attempt is made to achieve external validity or to quantify assessments. Indeed, in extending invitations to the authors to contribute to this volume, I asked them to subjectively, but rigorously, assess the success or failure of the innovations.

The chapter authors who were personally involved in the planning described do not necessarily endorse all of the innovations adopted in the institutions with which they were associated, since, in each case, many individuals contributed to the planning process. In addition, most institutions experimented with ideas that the planners were not always confident would work as planned but in the spirit of experimentation thought they should try. And, of course, chapter authors do not necessarily endorse all of the ideas and innovations attempted in other institutions represented in this volume.

In Chapter One, Robert C. Birney describes the creation of a unique private college in Massachusetts, which received guidance and support from four nearby colleges and universities. A key aspect of the Hampshire College plan was the placing of responsibility on students for development and management of their own education, leading to comprehensive examinations at two stages, capped by a thesis. Active learning was fostered through innovative curricula and the inquiry approach to learning, with heavy emphasis on independent study and seminars—virtually dethroning the traditional course. The college has been able to develop a culture, accepted by all segments of the academic community more than twenty years later, that supports its original mission.

In Chapter Two, Edward W. Weidner and William G. Kuepper tell of the establishment of an innovative institution of a different kind, a state university that accepted the challenge to try new ideas. This led to interdisciplinarity as the bedrock of the academic plan for the University of Wisconsin-Green Bay. The objective was to focus on the teaching of problem solving, drawing on as many disciplines as possible. The planners settled on the environment as a central theme, around which each student developed an interdisciplinary concentration (with the possibility of a disciplinary comajor), supported by a wide variety of learning opportunities and capped by an off-campus real-life experience and a follow-up on-campus seminar on the problem area.

In Chapter Three, Dean E. McHenry explains the founding of the Santa Cruz campus of the University of California System, modeled in part on Oxford and Cambridge. The objective was to create an institution that would provide the virtues of a small college with the resources and benefits of a research university. This led to a residential college plan, each college providing classrooms, dining and recreational facilities, a small library, and activities that foster a sense of community. Students take integrated general education courses in which they focus on getting to know their culture, as well as seminars and courses on selected topics in the colleges; however, most of the students' curriculum consists of courses offered through universitywide boards of studies.

In Chapter Four, James W. Hall and Richard F. Bonnabeau report on the establishment of Empire State College, a college without a traditional campus. Each of the forty regional learning locations throughout the state of New York is staffed with faculty mentors, who help students build individualized curricula, tailored to fit their particular objectives, and then devise plans for completing degree requirements. Empire State's innovations include individualized learning contracts, field study, credit for prior education and experience, and distance education, but its unique contribution to nontraditional education is its mentor-based approach to student academic planning and evaluation and an administrative structure to support it.

In Chapter Five, Alfred B. Chaet relates the saga of the University of West Florida, which also created residential colleges, though they differ markedly from the plan at the University of California, Santa Cruz. Three residential colleges, named Alpha, Gamma, and Omega, were established with the purpose of providing the sense of community sought in residential colleges but with a different academic plan. Traditional academic departments were assigned to the residential colleges in a way that ensured that each had one or more departments from each of the disciplinary areas—the humanities, social sciences, natural sciences, business, and education. As in the case of all of the other institutions described in this volume, teaching was given primacy over research in tenure, promotion, and financial rewards.

In Chapter Six, Robert C. Fox and Leah S. Harvey describe the founding of Metropolitan State University. The initial academic plan required students to devise their own bachelor's degree programs with the help of faculty advisers. One of the advisers' tasks was to persuade students, whose learning objectives were often vocational, to include liberal arts and sciences in their degree programs. In addition to resident faculty, community faculty are employed part-time, not primarily for cost reasons but to bring a practical dimension to student learning. Metro State does not have a traditional campus but uses available space all over the Minneapolis-Saint Paul area to teach classes. Public libraries are used to habituate students to lifelong learning.

In Chapter Seven, I recount the attempt of the University of Texas of the Permian Basin to experiment with a wide array of academic and administrative innovations. Founded as an upper-level institution (including master's degree programs), it discovered, as did Metro State, that only a minority of its undergraduate students come from community colleges. Primary emphasis was placed on teaching, mostly through conventional classes but including self-paced instruction, contract study, and field study. With a faculty who held Ph.D. degrees from the top graduate schools in the country, the university allowed them to decide whether they wished to be evaluated on research, and it employed a seven-year contract as an alternative to conventional tenure.

Why did some innovations fail and others prove less successful than anticipated or hoped? In some cases, the ideas were valid in theory but not in practice. In others, the innovations were not appropriate for the particular conditions—institution, state, time, and circumstance—under which they were tested.

A major factor was money. Many of the ideas required lower faculty-student ratios than were allowed by later funding; money was more abundant when the institutions were created and revision, if not complete elimination, of the original ideas was the inevitable course of action. Lack of equipment and facilities, usually due to lack of funds, played a role in some cases.

In a few cases, student attitudes became a consideration; however, of all the barriers to success, student acceptance appeared to be the least of the problems. Apparently, the overwhelming majority of students found the institutions and the innovations satisfactory. In most cases students knew a good deal about their institutions of choice before they enrolled, but in some cases students arrived unaware of the fact that they had enrolled in innovative schools employing practices quite different from those of most other colleges and universities.

Much as statistics tend to drift toward the mean, educational practices gravitate toward the traditional. This tendency can be traced to a variety of influences: accreditation, licensure and certification, new trustees, new faculty and administrators, community leaders, professional practitioners, students, and employers. Thus, the institutions examined in this volume, in attempting to try out new and nontraditional ideas, faced constant pressure to abandon the innovative and move toward the traditional. For example, at the University of Texas of the Permian Basin (UTPB), the designation Faculty of Earth Sciences was considered appropriate terminology by the planners and the faculty; although the program consisted primarily of geology, it also included oceanography, environmental studies, and geography. Nonetheless, geologists in the area—80 to 90 percent of whom lived in Midland near UTPB—constantly pressed to change the name to the Department of Geology, terminology familiar to them from their earlier days in college.

Many of the innovations failed or did not achieve the success envisioned by the planners due to turnover of administrations. New administrators were appointed who were not part of the original planning teams and did not agree with or did not place high value on the innovative practices. In some cases, only modest changes were made, but in others, major revisions were undertaken to bring the institutions into line with the norm.

Faculty, too, played a major role in these modifications, in some cases because they determined that the innovative ideas lacked validity or required more faculty time and energy than could reasonably be devoted to the associated activity. Several innovative institutions discovered that faculty who originally claimed to be attracted to the institutions because of the innovative plans were, within a year or two of employment, urging the institutions to make changes that conformed to their own previous experience—indeed, in some cases, to the practices of institutions that they had supposedly left because of insufficient innovation. But many of the faculty who sought a return to the traditional were appointed several years after the institutions were established. Some of these later faculty arrived without any commitment to the innovations that had attracted the original faculty to the institutions, and the newcomers gradually edged innovative ideas toward traditional practice.

The contributors to this volume are acutely aware of the difficulties of establishing and sustaining ideas that depart from the norm in higher education culture. As Chaet concludes in Chapter Five, it takes "a rare, imaginative individual, not a committee, to launch an innovative idea." While that claim may be debatable, it does remind us that the greatest changes in the organization, missions, and practices of higher education took place in the last quarter of the nineteenth century under the direction of strong administrators whose leadership styles would be anathema in today's academic world. In setting out on different paths, the founding presidents of many great universities changed American higher education: William Rainey Harper at the University of Chicago, Daniel Coit Gilman at Johns Hopkins, Andrew D. White at Cornell, G. Stanley Hall at Clark, and David Starr Jordan at Stanford. But substantive changes were also instituted at the same time in well-established institutions, most notably by Charles William Eliot, who in forty years (1869–1909) as president of Harvard introduced or presided over more innovations in American higher education than any single administrator before or since and created the preeminent model for the twentieth-century American university.

The institutions discussed in this volume are not necessarily the most innovative colleges and universities established during the 1960s and 1970s. They were selected because they represent the variety of innovations introduced during that period. Numerous other institutions also broke new ground in exploring alternatives to traditional higher education, among them Governors State University and Sangamon State University in Illinois; New College in Sarasota, now a component of the University of South Florida; the State University of New York College at Old Westbury; the College for Human Services in New York City; John F. Kennedy University in California; Oakland University and Grand Valley State College in Michigan; Richard Stockton State College, Ramapo College, and Thomas A. Edison State College in New Jersey; Simon's Rock College in Massachusetts; Evergreen State College in Washington State; Sonoma State University in California; and the State University of New York College at Utica-Rome.

Residential colleges constitute another category of experimental institutions established during the 1960s and early 1970s. These institutions were integral components of large universities but were given considerable autonomy and freedom to be innovative. Many were modeled after small, private liberal arts colleges. Examples are the Residential College at the University of Michigan, New College at the University of Alabama, Monteith College at Wayne State University, the three cluster colleges at the University of the Pacific, Fairhaven College at Western Washington University, Para College at Saint Olaf College, the ill-fated Bensalem College at Fordham University, and the three residential colleges at Michigan State University.

Finally, several long-established colleges instituted major innovations during this period that merit note, including Alverno College in Wisconsin, Mars Hill College in North Carolina, Colorado College, Tusculum College in Tennessee, Hiram College in Ohio, and Sterling College and Ottawa University in Kansas. This is, of course, an incomplete list, for dozens of established colleges and universities experimented with alternative approaches to the delivery and mission of higher education.

Although many of the innovations described in this volume did not work out as the planners anticipated and, in most cases, hoped, their impact on the vitality of the institutions involved was striking. The planners and initial faculty at each institution had a vision of something special that they wanted to accomplish academically, and that vision generated an extraordinary level of enthusiasm about their work. In most cases, this excitement was communicated to the students, who joined enthusiastically in the experiment. Almost all of the faculties say that the experiments were worth the effort, even if they were not total successes. A controlling principle for those who would experiment in academe: Never try to be innovative if failure is unacceptable.

V. Ray Cardozier
Editor

V. RAY CARDOZIER was founding vice president for academic affairs and for eight years the second president of the University of Texas of the Permian Basin. He is currently professor and director of the doctoral program in higher education at the University of Texas, Austin.

The curriculum of Hampshire College relies minimally on course-work, instead employing seminars, field study, contract study, and other approaches to inquiry through which students prepare for comprehensive examinations at three stages to qualify for a degree.

Hampshire College

Robert C. Birney

The innovator typically builds a new institution on a new model that replaces the old. The reformer revamps an existing institution to make it better. The traditionalist suspects them both of perfidy (Hefferlin, 1969).

The founding ideas for Hampshire College appear in *The New College Plan: A Proposal for a Major Departure in Higher Education* (Barber, Sheehan, Stoke, and McCune, 1958), written at the request of the presidents of Amherst College, Mount Holyoke College, Smith College, and the University of Massachusetts, with a grant from the Ford Foundation Fund for the Advancement of Education. Charles Longsworth has explained the presidents' thinking at that time.

> Let's go to the beginning. In 1958 the presidents of Amherst, Charles W. Cole; Mount Holyoke, Dick Gettell; the University of Massachusetts, Jean Paul Mather; and Smith, Benjamin Wright, received a proposal from four faculty who had been asked to think about a new college design. The proposal, called *The New College Plan, A Proposal for a Major Departure in Higher Education,* was prepared at a time when imminent growth in the college-age population put demands upon American colleges and universities to provide space and opportunity for a vastly enlarged body of students.
>
> That was the first reason for thinking about a new college. The existing colleges felt the pressure to grow and didn't want to. Charlie Cole told me that he thought Amherst (then a thousand; now 1,550) would lose its character.
>
> Further, the presidents thought the existing institutions working with a new college, might "develop new departures in educational methods and techniques."

That was the second reason. The presidents found their institutions resistant to change. They were successful, prestigious, conservative, and happy. Yet there were faculty and administrators and students who were restless, who thought there might be better ways to educate, that colleges could have a richer social life, that traditions should be challenged and broken. But these traditions were strong. As Dick Gettell of Mount Holyoke said in 1967, "We are not by definition schools that will run off at any new ideas." That was and is an accurate statement [Story, 1992, p. 109].

Harold Johnson, an Amherst alumnus, found the ideas appealing and pledged $6 million toward the estimated $12 million needed to create the new college. In 1965, the four college presidents joined Johnson on the board of trustees for the new Hampshire College, commissioned a revision of the 1958 plan, and hired Franklin Patterson as the founding president in the spring of 1966 and Charles Longsworth as vice president and treasurer. The four colleges, together with Hampshire College, became Five Colleges, Inc., an active consortium cooperating on a wide range of academic and administrative affairs. Planning, construction, and recruitment occupied the period from 1966 to 1970. The college opened in 1970 with an entering class of 251.

Patterson and Longsworth (1966) prepared *The Making of a College,* a 350-page "case statement" for Hampshire College, detailing every facet of the institution-to-be. The ideas expressed in the letter of transmittal (November 14, 1958) for the 1958 plan remained intact:

It is a widely held conviction among liberal arts faculties that our system of courses and credits has got out of hand, and that our students are capable of far more independence than they exercise in present college programs. We propose a college which frees both students and faculty from the system which makes education a matter of giving and taking courses to cover subjects.

At New College subjects will be covered, not by providing complete programs of courses, but by training students en masse to recognize fields of knowledge. The systematic and sustained effort will be made to train students to educate themselves. As freshmen they will start with seminars especially designed as the first step, not the last, in independence.

Other devices, such as student led seminars associated with all lecture courses will follow to reinforce this initial experience. Throughout, the program will provide for a type of social interaction which will create a climate favorable to intellectual activities.

Students will study only three courses at a time, an arrangement making possible concentration of effort and high levels of achievement. The faculty, on their side, will give only one lecture course at any given time; the rest of their energies will be devoted to the several kinds of seminars which characterize the curriculum. The student's program will be built on a large freedom of choice among areas of learning, and will be tested impersonally, by field examinations set according to recognized professional standards, frequently with the participation of outside examiners.

The college's total offering of lecture courses will be small. But it will be supplemented by other kinds of study and testing. It will also be supplemented to some degree by the collateral use of the course offerings of the sponsoring institutions and there will be each year a month-long mid-winter term after the Christmas vacation, during which the whole college will join in studying two courses which will provide a common intellectual experience.

The changes proposed will lead to significant economies in dollars, and more important, in the number of teachers required: we calculate that The New College Plan by giving up the attempt at a complete course offering (impossible for a college in any case), will make it possible for a faculty of fifty to give a first-rate education to 1,000 undergraduates. This ratio of 1 to 20 will go with efficient sizes of classes: relatively large groups in lectures and small groups in seminars. But the proposal has not been arrived at by cutting up the curriculum to fit economic considerations; on the contrary, educational motives have been paramount throughout our planning. Because the economies are motivated in this positive way, it seems to us they can actually be carried out.

We should add the several innovations we propose for New College, including in the extracurricular area the elimination of fraternities and inter-collegiate athletics in favor of more spontaneous forms of student recreation, are changes that would reinforce each other, so that a style of life should emerge at the college which would have its own momentum. This does not mean that we look to the establishment of a place which would appeal only to "special experimental" people, either as students or faculty. On the contrary, we are convinced that the time is ripe for a general shift in emphasis in first-rate liberal arts colleges, and that New College, working with a representative student body and faculty, could provide an example which would have wide influence.

This is a proposal for changes not in ends but in means. It affirms a belief in liberal arts education—that appropriate for a free man. Although New College aims at producing useful citizens, it rejects vocationalism and a narrow concentration on science divorced from humanism. The challenge of authoritarianism must not be met by a surrender of the principle that the supreme goal of an educational system is the free growth of the student and of the intellectual community.

If this report seems at times to be expressed with a conviction warranted by a proven experiment rather than an untried one, the authors may offer the compulsions of brevity as one reason for their forthright statement; but even more they must confess their enthusiasm for the plan as they wrestle with its philosophy and translate convictions into proposals. We earnestly hope that the project will be found a wise one, and that the necessary support can be enlisted to make "New College" a reality. Respectfully submitted, C. L. Barber, Amherst College, Donald Sheehan, Smith College, Stewart M. Stoke, Mount Holyoke College, Shannon McCune, University of Massachusetts, Chairman [Barber, Sheehan, Stoke, and McCune, 1958, pp. 3–5].

The Making of a College added two more important innovations as a consequence of the planners' deliberations: (1) faculty employment based on a renewable contract system rather than pursuit of tenure track careers and (2) the college offering little or no student financial aid. Neither financial aid considerations nor the employment-by-contract commitment had been considered in the 1958 plan. These were part of the planning when the college opened in 1970.

From the beginning, two contextual forces affected the college. First, Hampshire was and is a creation of the Five Colleges consortium in western Massachusetts. Its many dependencies on its neighbors were understood from the outset, despite its status as a financially independent, freestanding member of Five Colleges, Inc. Second, 1970 and the years following were not ordinary times in the life of the nation. The free speech movement at the University of California, Berkeley, in 1964, the military draft for an ill-defined war, the student riot and movement at Columbia University, and the death of students at Kent State in the spring of 1970 all combined to place the purposes and ideas of Hampshire on the "establishment" side of the ledger. The reforms in *The Making of a College* suddenly looked pallid indeed next to the blandishments of collectivism, communalism, and "power to the people." Very few of the education practices reviewed here were condemned out of hand as too radical at the time. Far from it, the new students at Hampshire College and many of the faculty considered them insufficiently radical to address the times. Oddly enough, since all five of the colleges in the consortium experienced these pressures, this period may have muted criticism and resistance to Hampshire's internal practices from neighboring faculty and students, who had their own hands full at home.

Economic Assumptions

Neither of the two economic assumptions about financial aid and the faculty-student ratio were ever realized. The ratio has never exceeded 1:14, and no one expects it to ever go higher. The 1966 projections for financial aid were greatly exceeded in 1970 and have been a major budgetary issue ever since. For a very long time the college operated with 85 percent of its revenues provided by tuition and fees. Strenuous efforts to raise endowments have generated a modest $10 million, which proved most valuable when flagging admissions in the mid-1980s required deficit operating budgets.

Academic Program: Progress by
Examination Versus Course Credits

Of the many departures from tradition at Hampshire College, the academic program consumed the lion's share of the planners' time and, in due course, presented the faculty and administration with some of their most difficult problems. Yet, it was the academic program that constituted the central focus of Hampshire's difference from traditional institutions and the essence of its justification.

It was the conviction of the planners that students could take charge of their education and accept greater responsibility for its definition and their means of pursuing it. In the fall of 1970, the entering students faced the following requirements for the bachelor's degree: (1) pass a Division One examination in each of the four schools of the college, (2) explore the possibilities of field study, taking time out, as well as enroll in courses in the neighboring institutions, (3) with the assistance of faculty advisers, make the necessary decisions to progress toward a degree, (4) accept personal responsibility for keeping the college's central records office fully informed about academic activities and achievements, (5) participate in all manner of study groups as well as the large lecture courses offered, and (6) by the third year, pass a Division Two concentration examination for admission into the final Division Three thesis requirement.

The decision to "dethrone the course" as the unit of educational progress produced a totally unexpected complication. Because the course credit is what tuition buys, we had inadvertently destroyed the cost basis of tuition. Students and parents quickly discovered this, and before long some students went on leave, stayed nearby, used the library, talked with advisers and teachers, and prepared for examinations on their own. What, they asked, was the fee for one Division One examination? Obviously, it would not equal a full semester's tuition! We concluded, just as obviously, that it did. But it posed a nice dilemma. If we were not selling credit hours, what were we selling? Examinations? Time on campus? Months of access to faculty and facilities? The latter is Hampshire's answer. Apparently, the credit hour plays a far more vital role in the economic health of colleges than most people recognize.

By the spring of 1974, most students had learned how to accept their responsibilities under the Hampshire type of program. The premise that they could do more learning than in a conventional program had proved valid. The consequence of their doing more, however, was that the faculty found themselves working much harder than they had ever worked before. Most of this work was serious intellectual activity and therefore enjoyably exhausting.

As the faculty's work load increased, they shifted increasingly more responsibility to the students. The students eventually were required to compose each Division One examination, propose it to the chair of the examination committee, whom they had recruited, fulfill the contract and schedule, and eventually pass the examination. The composition of the examination committee changed from faculty and outside examiners to a faculty chair assisted by advanced student examiners. The Division Two examination is composed by faculty, and outside examiners may join faculty for the Division Three examination, which leads to the awarding of the degree.

As the system worked increasingly well for those who understood it and were drawn into it, it began to increasingly work against those who could not become so engaged. The system required the students to express genuine intellectual interest in some aspect of their studies. A certain proportion of them discovered that they had no intellectual interests and could not manufacture them for purposes of progress by examination. One indicator in central records proved to be a reliable predictor of eventual student dropout, namely, failure to pass a single Division One examination by the end of the first year. Some students discovered they simply could not function well without grades and the comfort and satisfaction that getting grades gave them. These students transferred to other institutions. A sizable group of students found that there was an emotional cost in letting themselves embrace the intellectual creativity needed to be comfortable with and enjoy progress by examination. These people did pass some Division One examinations, but they eventually transferred out anyway.

Initially, the dropout rates for entering classes, as calculated against a four-year graduation rate, were a treacherously high 40 percent. This put the admissions officers under an extraordinary burden, since they had to recruit students at nearly twice the rate they had originally intended in order to maintain full enrollment.

By 1987, various efforts to reduce the attrition rates were still disappointing. At that point, the faculty agreed to let students substitute a one-year sequence of two courses in at least two schools of their choosing for a Division One examination. This modification marked the first time at Hampshire that the course as a unit of instruction was vested with value for progress toward the degree.

On a more positive note, it was clear not only that the faculty had learned how to teach the inquiry method so vital to the success of progress by examination but also that new faculty who had no personal history of involvement with the planning of the college could learn how to do it. Moreover, increasing numbers of entering students understand the contract system and the measurement of progress by examination and welcome the responsibilities that each entails.

The 1958 estimate that students can be more fully involved in their education proved valid. As Hampshire has witnessed, however, the consequences are profoundly adverse for those who cannot adapt to this nontraditional approach to college education.

Central Records

The requirement that students keep the central records office informed of their progress soon proved extremely difficult to sustain. Compliance by faculty and students varied across the spectrum in terms of speed, quality, and reliability. By 1987, it was necessary to invoke negative sanctions for faculty and a system of prompts for students in order to avoid the embarrassments caused by serious delinquencies in the maintenance of academic records. It is noteworthy that the originally anticipated difficulty of persuading graduate schools and employers to accept applicants' unconventional portfolios was, for most, far from insurmountable. A great many institutions have unconventional portfolios, and strong graduate and professional schools quickly learned that excellent students attend many of these institutions and thus that refusals to accept their portfolios might deny them outstanding graduates. Much work has gone into the streamlining, layout, and efficiency of the portfolio system, and it now seems clear that the portfolio gives a far more immediate and accurate picture of the quality and accomplishment of the student mind that produced it than does any array of credit hours and grade points.

Hampshire College graduates are welcome in the strongest academic departments and professional schools in the United States and abroad; they have performed extremely well in their graduate studies and often report having far better preparation for the independence required of graduate students than evidenced by classmates from conventional backgrounds.

One surprise regarding alumni was their ability as entrepreneurs, creating and sustaining their own business enterprises, nonprofit service organizations, and artistic programs. In hindsight, it is clear that responsibility for their own academic work prepared them for the challenges of establishing their own enterprises. Those with a profit orientation may prove to be a valuable resource for the college, as many of these people are loyal and attentive alumni.

Curriculum

At the outset the assumption was that the inquiry method of teaching could be adapted to any array of course content and faculty research interests because it aims at "the cultivation of student capacities for interpretation, discovery, creation, and the critical ability to recognize and understand the significance of competing theories and models" (Weaver, 1989, p. 6). This has proved to be the case. The assumption that Hampshire faculty would bring disciplinary emphases that complemented the offerings at the other colleges in the consortium has proved to be true from time to time. One of the primary apprehensions in the beginning was that Hampshire College students might place an unbearable burden on the neighboring institutions as they flocked to them to take exchange courses. Current data show that Hampshire students take a few more of their courses at the neighboring institutions than was originally planned (24 percent versus 20 percent). Exchange rates wax and wane with intellectual fashion, but by and large they stay within manageable limits and on balance contribute to a lively diversity of viewpoints in the classroom.

In 1970, the Program of Language and Communication was considered a bold experiment in curriculum design for undergraduates. In 1972, it became a probationary school with the provision that a thorough review and recommendation be performed in 1980. In 1985, the fourteen faculty members of the school representing modern communications, computer science, philosophy, and cognitive psychology were given permanent status, and the name was changed to the School of Communications and Cognitive Science. This is an excellent illustration of the flexibility of the school model devoted to field presentations by faculty drawn from a variety of allied disciplines.

The most recent curriculum innovation was highly controversial at the time of its proposal and eventual passage, but it now seems well accepted by the faculty and students. Known as the Third World Perspective, it consists of a resolution passed by the faculty:

> Hampshire College is committed to the principle that a student's education is incomplete without an intellectual engagement with the experiences of the peoples of Asia, Africa, and Latin America (including North America's domestic "third world"). As in the study of other areas of the world, this naturally includes issues of gender. For both the intrinsic importance of such knowledge and the instrumental importance of understanding multiple perspectives, the college expects each student to present tangible evidence, prior to graduation, that such engagement has occurred. Under normal conditions, this will take place in division two and in the context of the planning design of a concentration.

Although this resolution addresses the student's obligation, the burden on the faculty for teaching and advising is clear. Obviously, many different interpretations are advanced by faculty members, but at the heart of the resolution is the proposition that there is value in the study and mastery of diverse perspectives across cultures, ethnic groups, and genders. The requirement seems to be functioning well and constitutes an extraordinary general education initiative.

To summarize the Hampshire academic program, curriculum, and faculty contribution, it appears that student responsibility for personal learning is based on positive incentives that draw students into their studies. And the faculty have learned that the inquiry method of teaching supports, enhances, and stimulates their own research interests.

The greatest single hazard in the system involves identification of those students who deny their inability to progress and erect a variety of smoke screens to hide their academic inactivity. The advising relationship is all-important here and requires proactive behavior from faculty. Clearly, this kind of advising does not always occur, so a wider net of residence advisers, house masters, and others has to be employed to reach out to students who retreat from their studies.

Schools Versus Departments

The present organization of Hampshire College clearly reflects the commitment to interdisciplinary activity. By grouping the faculty into fields of interests, as opposed to departments, disciplines are represented in two or more schools, and the opportunity to appoint a new faculty member often has led to the selection of someone from a discipline not yet represented. The value of this arrangement is reinforced by the intellectual demands of the examination system, wherein committee members are selected for the different disciplinary perspectives that they offer to the students. From 1970 to the present, a period in which both expansion and contraction of the number of faculty positions occurred, the flexibility of this disciplinary mix has sustained the progress-by-examination system and fostered inter-disciplinary research and teaching by the faculty. More often than not the emphasis has been on complementarity of interests rather than reinforcement of specific interests through increased numbers of faculty within a single discipline.

One other development over the years is noteworthy, namely, the progressive downgrading of authoritative leadership as embodied in deanships and the like. The founding deans, and their immediate successors, were appointed partly because of the planners' belief that the schools needed strong leadership. Subsequently, each school has opted to assign the deans' duties to faculty members, who serve limited terms carrying out the organizational duties of the deanery.

Employment by Contract

The original employment-by-contract decision for faculty was made after consultation with the American Association of University Professors representatives, who gave assurances that, for them, academic freedom was to be found in the practices of the institution and not solely in the faculty tenure system, although they viewed the latter as indispensable. Throughout the subsequent twenty-three years, numerous challenges to the employment-by-contract system have occurred. Nevertheless, it remains firmly in place at Hampshire College because it seems to meet the needs of both faculty and students. From the outset, the governance ideology of the college mandated broad participation in any assessment of the contract renewal process, including student input, student representatives on the contract review committees, and a wide net of information gathering around each renewal at the end of three years, at the end of five years, and so forth. All of this proved to be extremely burdensome, emotionally demanding, and, at times, quite divisive in the life of the schools and the college at large.

Over the years, the process has become more streamlined, systems have been developed to assist those who are preparing to petition for renewal, and, in the case of those who are standing for their third appointment, the renewal is for a period of ten years. With these modifications, it may appear that Hampshire has approached a tenure system, wherein persons who have been renewed through six years are eligible for a tenure appointment after which they are not further assessed in any formal, collegewide way. But, in fact, school deans conduct midterm reviews of all contracts, and the ten-year appointment still entails a midcareer or late-career formal renewal in which the fifteen- to twenty-year faculty member is presented with questions about vitality and continued commitment.

There have been instances of difficult, even bitterly fought, reappointment cases, resulting in either of the two possible outcomes. However, the experience with the contract system has been that persons who are not likely to secure reappointment frequently choose not to stand for reappointment. This choice is made for a variety of reasons, but it permits a reasonably graceful departure by any individual who has failed to perform well in the Hampshire College system. Nevertheless, despite the stress that the system can induce, those who have been a part of it for a long time continue to reject periodic proposals for a tenure system.

Governance

Probably no general area of inquiry has been so vexing as the questions pertaining to governance and the power to commit money in the name of the college. The original model of the college defined an incorporated, not-for-profit, freestanding education institution with a hierarchy of strong, experienced leadership. From the outset, there was a strong challenge to this model, which emphasized community spirit, an open process of decision making, and the necessity of maintaining high levels of consensus. A hybrid form of government almost immediately began to emerge in which the formal hierarchical model was matched by an interlocking network of large committees representing constituencies given to general meetings.

The post of dean of the college was redefined as dean of the faculty. Responsibility for student life is now under a dean of student affairs after more discursive handling by the house masters designated in the residence system, and the president is assisted by a standing committee of unit heads who are expected to share with their constituencies the issues that have been brought forth for action. The overall style of government was born with high levels of citizen participation, and to this day the college continues to emphasize openness of action and consensual politics.

Student Life

The faculty planners of the late 1960s at Hampshire College spent much time on the design of the residence system in the hope and belief that both architecture and organization could provide students with experience in the arts of citizenship that would serve both them and their nation well in the turbulent times ahead. When the college opened, the house master system was initiated with the expectation that full-time faculty members would reside with their families in the dormitories, direct their staffs in the creation of valuable social programs, and provide the linkage needed to ensure the individual student ample and accurate access to professional counseling and health services. The master system was eliminated, as it became clear that well-qualified faculty should not be recruited to manage residential life. They were eventually replaced by persons whose professional orientations attracted them to student life management. That has evolved into a system of resident managers who report to a dean of student affairs in the conventional manner found throughout American higher education. Of all the aspirations delineated at the outset for what might be accomplished in this area of the college, it is fair to say that the failure of the residence system was essentially total. The present residential life system at Hampshire College is probably neither better nor worse than that of any strong liberal arts college in the country.

Outdoor Program

In 1958, the planners concluded that intercollegiate athletics should not have a place in the New College. The assumption that Hampshire College would do best by allowing club sports to wax and wane has proved wholly valid. The census records of daily use of the athletic facilities show that a high proportion of Hampshire students take responsibility for their own physical education. Students join outdoor clubs, canoe and kayak clubs, and rock-climbing clubs, play tennis, and indulge in various other forms of intramural team sports. Student satisfaction with the athletic facilities and their administration has always been reasonably high, and any dissatisfaction expressed has always been motivated by a desire for more and better facilities. Just what the absence of a sizable community of varsity athletes means to the quality of life at Hampshire will probably never be known. But there is no question that such students, in any large numbers, are absent.

Hampshire College Today

Many of the students who matriculate at Hampshire College have little or no understanding of the special nature of the program. For many others, Hampshire is their only choice. Many of the new faculty come with a sense of excitement at securing a fine appointment, but with no predilections about the value and uniqueness of the teaching environment that they are about to enter. Nevertheless, all parties soon settle in, and we have seen successive generations adapt to and appreciate the Hampshire College program. There is no question that for the engaged student Hampshire is a very challenging place. There is also no question that those who drop out do so for honest intellectual reasons.

The quality of work done at the college is intellectually strong. And unlike many colleges, the student body, as well as the faculty, is composed of demonstrably sensitive and socially responsible people who try hard to make a difference in their campus community, the surrounding community, and the world at large. This social commitment is well illustrated by the proportion of graduates who enter government, education, not-for-profit service, and all manner of social service organizations. There is no question that the spirit of experimentation is alive and well. The degree of self-assessment and self-preoccupation is probably no higher than that found at many institutions of quality. But thanks to the system employed at Hampshire, there is a high level of flexibility and adaptiveness that the college continues to put to good use.

The planners expressed the hope in 1958 that the work done at the New College would be recognized and valued by others in higher education. Charles Longsworth has offered his thoughts on how things have turned out.

Has Hampshire fulfilled the dreams of its founders? In the 1962 study *More Power to Them: A Report of Faculty and Student Experience in the Encouragement of Student Initiative* [Barber, 1962], there is an introductory statement: "This report will describe one among several current projects aimed at countering the tendency of our undergraduates to leave too much of the initiative in their education in the hands of their teachers."

Assuming student initiative to be a good thing, has Hampshire encouraged it?

Here are quotations from a 1990 study of Hampshire by the Higher Education Research Institute at UCLA, one of the highly respected ongoing research efforts in higher education, the source of the freshman attitude studies you have seen for many years. "The major findings from the study of Hampshire College alumni suggest that the Hampshire experiment has been a very successful one. Early on, Hampshire had the vision to identify mechanisms through its structure and curriculum that encourage active learning—the kind of learning that is viewed today as one of the most essential ingredients in a successful undergraduate experience. We believe that Hampshire provides a model of active learning that can be emulated in many key respects by other institutions of higher education."

In several other ways Hampshire is different from colleges with which it is directly compared or which may be familiar to you. The following are relative statements summarizing the characteristics of Hampshire College graduates and comparing them with the graduates of a New England coeducational college of high quality:

• Hampshire has engaged nonscience students, especially women students who have avoided science, in the sciences and mathematics.
• Hampshire has encouraged and fostered growth in the capacity to work and think independently. This is frequently noted by graduates. Some who have experienced graduate school remark that they were not as well prepared factually as their contemporaries from other schools, but were better prepared in how to search and evaluate evidence, ask questions, and trust their own judgment.
• Hampshire graduates are more likely to pursue careers in public service, become entrepreneurs, participate in social and community organizations, and be involved in politics or civil rights, give money to causes in which they believe, etc. In other words to be active, involved citizens.
• Hampshire has developed a collaborative, learning faculty that is highly productive, and has created a culture that is very supportive of the institution's mission to develop active learners with a strong social consciousness.

So there is evidence that the Hampshire College experiment is successful and has achieved a result that distinguishes it from other colleges.

There were disappointments. Bob Birney pointed to the largest in a recent conversation. It was a result of the naivete with which we began Hampshire College. We really believed we could make a difference, not just in the lives of our graduates, but in the world. We thought that Hampshire, if successful, would, as Sandy and Helen Astin say in the Higher Education Research Institute report, "provide a model of active learning that can be emulated in many key respects by other institutions of higher education." Sadly, one thing institutions do not do is learn much from each other. The wheel is continuously reinvented. Dick Gettell was right, not in speaking about Mount Holyoke, but in general about colleges: "We are not by definition schools that will run off at any new ideas."

The difference today, as compared with twenty-five years ago, is in the more widely shared view of the value of independence of mind, of the usefulness of multidisciplinary study to understand complex problems, of the need for talent in socially important work, of the significance of the ongoing problem of injustice, of the failure of our institutions to teach science for citizens, of the waste when talented women avoid science, of the significance of new fields of knowledge, of new combinations of disciplines, of the changes in known fields, of the utility of technology in most fields! These are all issues Hampshire has addressed with some considerable success. Other institutions also are struggling with those issues. We need to share our new understandings. But sharing is offering and accepting. No institutions of any kind in this country have a worse case of the "not invented here" syndrome than have our colleges and universities. It is amazing how compartmentalized, provincial, and egocentric colleges can be [Story, 1992, pp. 126–127].

Hampshire's influence on higher education can be measured by the steadily rising rates of inquiry from other institutions, its growing number of alumni who serve on the faculties of major universities, and public recognition by teaching educators. Perhaps change in higher education is generational at best, and Hampshire's contributions lie ahead.

References

Barber, C. L. *More Power to Them: A Report of Faculty and Student Experience in the Encouragement of Student Initiative.* Amherst, Mass.: Committee for New College, 1962.

Barber, C. L., Sheehan, D., Stoke, S. M., and McCune, S. *The New College Plan: A Proposal for a Major Departure in Higher Education.* Amherst, Mass.: The Four Colleges, 1958.

Hefferlin, J. B. *The Dynamics of Academic Reform.* San Francisco: Jossey-Bass, 1969.

Patterson, F., and Longsworth, C. R. *The Making of a College.* Cambridge, Mass.: Massachusetts Institute of Technology Press, 1966.

Story, R. (ed.). *Five Colleges: Five Histories.* Amherst, Mass.: Five Colleges, Inc., and Historic Deerfield, Inc., 1992.

Weaver, F. S. "Liberal Education, Inquiry, and Academic Organization." In F. S. Weaver (ed.), *Promoting Inquiry in Undergraduate Learning.* New Directions for Teaching and Learning, no. 38. San Francisco: Jossey-Bass, 1989.

ROBERT C. BIRNEY *was founding dean of the School of Social Sciences and later vice president of Hampshire College, Amherst, Massachusetts. He now resides in Williamsburg, Virginia.*

Curricula are built around interdisciplinary concentrations in this new university, and although some of the other original aspirations have faded twenty-five years later, most students continue to major in interdisciplinary programs.

University of Wisconsin-Green Bay

Edward W. Weidner, William G. Kuepper

Colleges and universities experienced a period of unprecedented growth in the 1960s. The rapid increase in the number of students wishing to pursue higher education led to more restrictive admissions, a tremendous expansion of the size of state universities, and a substantial addition to the number of colleges and universities. And criticism abounded.

Criticism of American Universities

In the mid-1960s, higher education was frequently criticized for insufficient relevance, although those making the charge were not always certain as to what constituted relevance. Many observers argued that emphasis on graduate work and research meant neglect of undergraduate teaching. Graduate work was largely in the disciplines, and, it was alleged, this monopoly helped the disciplines control each university. The basic unit of organization of the universities was the disciplinary departments. As a result, interdisciplinarity and the study of problems that transcended disciplinary lines were difficult to pursue.

In the mid-1960s, a sharp debate focused on general education. In particular, universities drew criticism for defining general education as a distribution requirement, or as a series of freshman or sophomore courses in the regular disciplines. As a result, there was much experimentation with general education requirements. Some of these involved expansion of American studies, international studies, and the study of the humanities and non-Western cultures.

Some critics called for diversity in the curriculum; others thought that diversity in the curriculum could be achieved through independent study; still others suggested that there should be diversity in grading, electives, majors, living accommodations, and types of colleges or schools. Observers urged increased choices for students across as well as within institutions, whether large or small. Faculty and administrators tried residential colleges, cluster colleges, living-learning arrangements, honors programs, and other experiments.

The relationship between professor and student also was scrutinized. There was an overwhelming feeling that at the undergraduate level this relationship had become distant, as professors relegated undergraduate instruction to teaching assistants. Overall, critics charged, relationships of professors to undergraduates were largely transitory and impersonal. The faculty and students seemed to be developing separate cultures.

The University of Wisconsin in the Mid-1960s

Higher education in Wisconsin in the 1960s reflected national trends. Enrollment was soaring. What had started out more than a century earlier as the University of Wisconsin at Madison had expanded well beyond the initial campus. Through statewide extension, and, after World War II, through freshman-sophomore centers located in many of the state's larger cities, the university had a direct impact in all regions of the state. A second major campus was added in Milwaukee during the 1950s and eventually given autonomous status within the University of Wisconsin. To better accommodate this change, President Fred Harvey Harrington shifted to a university chancellor system. Thus, by the time the governor signed the law authorizing the University of Wisconsin-Green Bay (UWGB) in September 1965, the University of Wisconsin System was prepared both organizationally and procedurally to add the new campus to its cluster.

The university system was not entirely free, however, to do what it wished with the new campus. The Coordinating Council for Higher Education had been created to exercise supervisory authority over the three systems of higher education in the state, which included the Wisconsin state universities (the former state teachers colleges) and the Vocational, Technical, and Adult Educational System, as well as the University of Wisconsin. University of Wisconsin central administration officials felt that relations with the coordinating council could be made easier if the new university at Green Bay were innovative, not directly duplicating the educational opportunities available at state university institutions.

Thus, some of the constraints that affected the new university were clear. First, it was to be a public university, subject to the various political pressures that are a part of any state system of higher education. Second, UWGB would be part of a system, not an independent university with its own board of regents. Third, the University of Wisconsin System would compete with the Wisconsin State University System for students and funds. These restraints made innovation all the harder to institute at UWGB.

Developing the Principles of the Academic Plan

The first chancellor of UWGB, appointed in October 1966, was given five months to develop the preliminary academic plan for review by the Office of the President and by the University of Wisconsin Board of Regents. He was given only seventeen months to develop a complete academic plan under which the new university would operate. With this kind of time pressure, and with the request for innovation at the new university, the new chancellor and his advisers examined the problems and promises of American higher education in the 1960s.

The preliminary academic plan was, of necessity, largely the product of only a few persons, since there was no time to recruit even a sample faculty. As the chancellor recruited faculty members, more persons could participate in the development of the academic plan. While this procedure provided substantial disadvantages, it also offered an important advantage: The model or plan could be presented to a prospective faculty member as an incentive for joining the new endeavor. Consequently, most of the faculty members who accepted appointments at the new university were committed to the preliminary academic plan. In due time, this commitment permitted a hiring, merit increase, promotion, and faculty governance system congruent with the innovative orientation of UWGB. Moreover, as the small group of professors worked on perfecting the academic plan, an innovative model, rather than just a series of innovations, gradually evolved.

New universities have recognition problems. Most go through a hazing period, during which questions are raised about their quality and role. At least a partial solution to the problem of recognition seemed available to UWGB. Its comprehensive innovative model might serve to stimulate innovation at other universities in the United States and, indeed, in other countries. If this influence was realized, it would bring favorable attention to the new university and thereby enhance its recognition and reduce hazing problems in Wisconsin.

In addition, planners thought that UWGB, as a new university, had an obligation to try new, different ideas, particularly ideas that an established university would find difficult to embrace. Thus, professors at Green Bay were advised by their counterparts at Madison to emphasize interdisciplinarity, which was difficult or impossible to achieve on the Madison campus.

Interdisciplinarity became the bedrock of the academic plan early on. In part, this stemmed from a problem approach to learning. The plan emphasized that students could be enriched by focusing on the many facets of real-world problems and that problem solving required contributions from many disciplines. Which themes should be emphasized by the new university? Gradually, two pairs emerged: the biophysical environment and the social environment, on the one hand, and how individuals influence and are influenced by their environment, on the other. If an interdisciplinary approach to problem solving was adopted, then environment as a general theme for the university seemed appropriate. Some planners criticized this focus, however, arguing that it might be so broadly construed as to be meaningless, or that it should simply be one focus and not *the* focus. Still, the environmental focus was accepted as an institutional emphasis and, more specifically, as a way to pursue a problem-solving orientation to learning.

Initially, the university planners proposed four theme colleges to encourage interdisciplinarity within their bounds. But as discussion of the academic plan continued, this design was seen as an inadequate way to ensure interdisciplinarity. As a result, units called concentrations were instead proposed as the central organizing mechanisms. They were to be problem-oriented and interdisciplinary. Disciplines were to be subordinate and supportive. Students would have to choose a concentration in which to major, but they could also choose a discipline in which to comajor. Faculty members would have to choose a concentration as their official home. The concentrations were given authority over budget, curriculum, assignments of faculty, appointing power, merit increases, and promotions. They thus served as the UWGB analogue of the academic department. Gradually, the concentration became more important than the theme college—in part because of construction restrictions on the campus and in part because of the surplus organization created by having several colleges.

Along with interdisciplinarity, a highly integrated general education program, the Liberal Education Seminars, was basic to the UWGB academic plan. Almost all of the principles of educational philosophy represented in the academic plan were found in some measure within this program. The Liberal Education Seminars were designed to treat education not as a set of beginning disciplinary courses, crammed in at the freshman and sophomore levels, but rather as something more distinctive, spread throughout a student's four years.

The academic plan called for each theme college to offer one or more sequences of seminars in particular problem areas, such as water resources or transportation. The freshman seminar would be an initial, campus-based, in-depth examination of a problem. As a sophomore, a student would engage in an off-campus experience in northeastern Wisconsin, followed by a seminar discussion designed to explore the meaning of the experience. As a junior, the student, after appropriate orientation, would go to another subculture in the United States or abroad to study the same theme or problem in a different context. Again, a seminar discussion would follow the field experience. As a senior, the student would enroll in a seminar stressing the interrelation of the particular problem on which he or she had been focusing to other problems, across theme college lines.

The early planners realized that this seminar plan defined an ideal scenario that could not always be achieved. Most students would not want to stay with one set of problems for four years. And most students would be unable to go abroad. Still, the seminars could be used as a means to stimulate students in their assimilation of specific pieces of information, their observations, their thought processes, their values, and their ideas about the future.

Another aspect of the Liberal Education Seminars was that improvement in students' oral and written communication skills would be handled as a part of the freshman seminar, rather than treated separately in a freshman English course. To some degree, this model anticipated later initiatives in writing in the content area and writing across the curriculum.

To facilitate the practice of these innovations, UWGB adopted a 4-1-4 calendar. The one-month interim (January) would be used for off-campus projects focusing on the local area, as well as for travel abroad or to other parts of the North American continent. It also provided the opportunity for the development of one-time, unique courses not appropriate for the regular semesters.

Along with interdisciplinarity and general education, a cluster of items in the academic plan of UWGB directly addressed the role of students. There would be opportunities for experiential learning, individualization of learning, and student initiative education. Overall, there would be close student-professor relationships and the students would play central roles in their own academic plans and education.

Experiential learning was encouraged by the 4-1-4 calendar, as well as by numerous opportunities for students to work with community groups. Individualization of learning was encouraged by having students develop their own sets of requirements for graduation. Indeed, in the early years of the university, departments were discouraged from developing checklists of requirements for graduation. Student initiative education was encouraged by promoting the use of many independent study courses and even by enabling students, under faculty guidance, to develop their own courses. And, overall, the university hired professors who were very oriented toward teaching as their first responsibility. This would lead, it was hoped, to close student-professor relationships, especially since the university would have buildings that provided many places for students and faculty to get together.

There was much discussion about the regional obligations of UWGB. The term *communiversity* was coined to describe the ideal symbiotic interaction between the institution and the community. The regional role of the new university was further defined by the administrative attachment of three freshman-sophomore centers in the area. The goal was to integrate the curriculum, faculty, and staff of each center with those of the university.

At the same time, care was taken both at the campus level and at the University of Wisconsin System level to not label UWGB as just a regional university. The institutions of the University of Wisconsin System, while serving the needs of regional communities, would have broad statewide and even national and international responsibilities. That this role for UWGB was not universally accepted became very clear in 1967 when the Coordinating Council for Higher Education indicated that it supported the central rationale for establishing the new campus: to provide excellent liberal arts education opportunities on a regional basis for students within a radius of fifty to seventy-five miles. In contrast, the officially approved preliminary academic plan of UWGB stated that the institution would be a unit of the statewide University of Wisconsin System, focusing on the needs, problems, and activities of people residing in the northern Great Lakes area.

In February 1968, the academic plan was officially approved. The university was to be interdisciplinary in a problem-focused manner, with a distinctive form of general education and a strong emphasis on the student's role in learning. In many ways, the plan constituted a model for change that might be approached but never fully achieved.

The Doors Open

The university admitted its first students in the fall of 1968, and one year later began to move onto its new campus. The first years were heady for the new university. Many of the first students thrived on the academic innovations, which they had helped design. They were caught up in a period of rapid campus growth and considerable national attention on the university.

The environmental movement was riding high, and UWGB was riding high with it. Conferences on population and several other environmental issues attracted prominent scholars and political leaders to Green Bay. The university's general education contained a considerable dose of topics on the environment, many of its majors included a distinct environmental perspective, and its programs in the environmental sciences were strong from the start. Students and faculty were active in educational programs and community activities in support of environmental concerns, including Green Bay's first recycling program.

Articles began appearing in publications in the United States and abroad highlighting UWGB's curriculum innovation and environmental focus. *Harper's* said, "Survival U. is alive and well in Green Bay, Wisconsin." It described the university as "light-years ahead from anything ever tried in Wisconsin or elsewhere." Later, in what turned out to be a mixed blessing, *Newsweek* labeled the university, "Ecology U." The university's image was being fixed not only in the national education community but also in the region in which it was located and from which it drew most of its students.

Other than the substantial amount of attention that UWGB was attracting, little else came easily. During its early years, major problems arose. First, and most pervasive, the two systems of higher education in Wisconsin were merged, beginning a process of increasing homogenization among the state's thirteen public universities. Second, enrollment shortfalls in the 1970s began to result in erosion of the institutional budget. Third, on the curriculum front, it quickly became apparent that the Liberal Education Seminars, a very visible part of institutional innovation, could not be sustained in their pristine form.

Merger

The merger of the state's two university systems, completed in 1974 and attended by "productivity" budget cuts instituted by the governor, had a profound effect on UWGB. The anticipated cost savings that justified the merger were heavily dependent on decreases in the costs per student at the campuses of the former University of Wisconsin System—decreases designed to bring the costs closer to those at the institutions of the former state university system. UWGB's chancellor warned of the potential for "a sterile homogenization and sameness" within the new university system.

UWGB, facing a loss of funds under the merger, hoped for a reprieve based on its innovative academic plan. As part of the merger process, each of the fifteen institutions was directed to develop a new mission statement for approval by the board of regents. UWGB argued successfully that on the basis of its innovative approach to undergraduate education, it was sufficiently distinct from the remainder of the nondoctoral institutions to be recognized as a "special mission" university, one of only two institutions in the system so designated. Unfortunately for the university, the special designation was not accompanied by special funding. The net result was a sustained reduction in the level of UWGB resources, below what had been anticipated during the planning of the university and prior to discussions of merger.

The merger also brought an end to any lingering hopes that a multicampus university in northeast Wisconsin would have the chance to succeed. Undertaken to reduce costs and increase efficiency, the merger ironically served to set back the fundamentally sound multicampus approach to public higher education that was part of the UWGB design.

Liberal Education Seminars

A number of students who enrolled at UWGB in 1968 already had achieved junior standing, in part through coursework at the Green Bay two-year center that went out of business when the university opened and at three centers in the region that became administratively attached to UWGB. These students wanted to become, in two years, the first graduates of the new university. In accepting these students as juniors, the university committed itself to offering upper- as well as lower-division work the year that it opened its doors.

This decision further complicated an already major challenge to the faculty in curriculum development. Nowhere was this challenge more dramatically manifest than in the Liberal Education Seminars.

The task of staffing the Liberal Education Seminars was a challenge from the outset. Although the freshmen seminars had a small cadre of faculty hired to work in that program, the sophomore and junior seminars were organized at the discretion of the departments and of the deans. Their enthusiasm for the seminars was hardly uniform, and this variation was reflected in the attitudes toward and resources devoted to the program.

The goal of having significant numbers of students engaged in off-campus projects was the first component of the Liberal Education Seminars to be seriously compromised. Costs were high, and student enthusiasm was mixed. A number of schemes to avoid meeting this requirement soon emerged. In the early 1970s, academic advising produced a booklet, titled *How to,* that achieved a fair degree of notoriety, especially among supporters of the seminars. The booklet detailed several ways of avoiding various degree requirements through substitution and petition and symbolized the extent of discomfort felt by some students and faculty with the more unusual aspects of the university's academic plan.

Subsequent modifications of the seminar requirements proved insufficient to save the program. Despite some outstanding successes in the program and strong allegiance in some quarters, overall support wavered. When the late 1970s brought continued enrollment and budget problems, general education became the focus of the first of two major curriculum overhauls that were to profoundly affect the university.

Enrollment Problems and Curriculum Changes

Enrollment shortfalls at the university in the 1970s were by no means restricted to UWGB. But, by mid-decade, the failure to achieve enrollment projections called for remediation. A major study completed in early 1976 identified significant recruitment and retention difficulties. Among several issues, academic terminology was seen as pretentious and unfamiliar. In addition, the general education requirements were described as unwieldy, and many of the courses that fulfilled these requirements were seen as unrelated to students' academic goals at UWGB and untransferable if students completed degrees elsewhere. Later that year, plans to address these difficulties were laid out in a landmark remedial action plan—called the Logan-Murphy Report after its two faculty authors—for the institution.

The arrival of a new dean for academic affairs in 1977 provided the opportunity for a sweeping change in general education. Only a semester of the senior component of the Liberal Education Seminars survived in a new thirty-credit set of general education requirements. Supporters of the seminars concluded they would be better served by trying to influence the new requirements rather than by defending the old plan. The new approach was designed to retain important concepts of the Liberal Education Seminars while looking more like conventional general education requirements.

This action was the first of the two major curriculum changes at the university viewed by some faculty as a retreat from institutional values and a weakening of institutional distinctiveness. The second change, in 1984, was a redefinition of the university's majors and minors or, as the change is sometimes described, the introduction of disciplinary majors. This latter change was the result of careful comparisons of student transcripts with program descriptions and was intended to more accurately portray the curriculum of the university and the programs of study actually followed by students. For example, prior to 1984, a student could major in the interdisciplinary program Communication and the Arts and comajor in music. Following essentially the same curriculum after 1984, the student could major in music and minor in Communication and the Arts. As part of this change in program definitions, the program in business administration was formally identified as interdisciplinary. This allowed a student to major in business without taking an interdisciplinary "collateral," although the program continued to demand the completion of an outside field of study for its graduates by requiring a minor.

In addition to these curriculum modifications, a new degree-completion program in nursing (B.S.N.) was introduced, as was a degree in social work (B.S.W.). These new programs, clearly put in place to address regional needs, were seen, along with the curriculum changes, as a weakening of the university's commitment to a distinctive academic plan and, especially, to interdisciplinarity.

The view that interdisciplinarity was undermined by these changes was not uniformly held. The business faculty, for example, argued that the broadly stated requirements in the business administration major made the program strongly interdisciplinary. And faculty in the new B.S.W. program made extensive use of the liberal arts in designing the curriculum, a point highlighted by accreditation teams as a strength of the program. Throughout these and subsequent changes, the linchpin of interdisciplinarity at UWGB remained in place: the interdisciplinary department.

Meeting Regional Needs

In the 1980s, an increased emphasis on the professional programs and other curriculum changes characterized the open strategy to meet the educational needs of the region. This goal was reinforced with the arrival of the institution's second chancellor in 1986. The Faculty Senate, anticipating the search for the new chancellor, passed a resolution reaffirming the importance of "institutional distinctiveness," and the position posting emphasized the interdisciplinary, liberal arts mission of the university.

Upon his arrival, the new chancellor, while supporting the university's distinctiveness, used terms such as "comprehensive, urban university" and the university's "first obligation" to serve the region. Reservations still remained at UWGB about the merger, especially in regard to how it was leading to an undesirable homogeneity among the institutions. This concern about homogeneity and the curriculum changes that had already occurred resulted in opposition to the notion of regional service and to the identification of UWGB as a regional university.

Enrollment in the 1980s

Enrollment soared in the 1980s. An approximately 40 percent increase occurred in the first half of the decade, after enrollment had bottomed out in 1976–1977 and in 1977–1978. In addition to the program and nomenclature changes effected by the university, two other major developments appeared to drive the enrollment increases.

The first was the expansion of student housing to eleven hundred beds, equally divided between apartments and more traditional residence halls. A noticeable difference in on-campus activities began to occur in 1980 when, after years of negotiation, the university acquired the privately owned student apartments located on campus. Over the next five years, through private fundraising and financing, the capacity of on-campus housing was doubled.

The second development was the move from National Collegiate Athletic Association Division II to Division I. Although difficult times attended this transition, the move significantly reinforced institutional distinctiveness, since UWGB remains the only nondoctoral institution in the state that competes in Division I.

The enrollment increases of the early 1980s arrested the erosion of institutional funding that characterized the 1970s but did not result in an increase in resources directed to the campus. The investment per student continued to plummet from what the university system administrators argued was an intolerably high level during the 1970s to a level that, by 1985, approximated the average for the nondoctoral universities in the system.

UWGB's experimental look and its early enrollment struggles had created skepticism among senior system officials that the campus would ever achieve significant growth. By the time the university was experiencing that growth, enrollment funding had disappeared, resources available to the university system had not kept pace with enrollment increases, and system administrators were reluctant to move funds from one campus to another.

Enrollment Management

In 1986, in an attempt to maintain academic quality and as part of a deal cut with Wisconsin's governor to bring resources more closely in line with the number of students served, the university system began reducing its enrollment. In recognition of the fact that UWGB was undersized and thus unable to adequately serve its region, it was the only institution given permission to grow during the second phase of the management scheme (by fifty full-time equivalent students for four years). As if to prove the extent of the enrollment pressure it was experiencing, the university exceeded its four-year authorized increase in the first fall term.

This large increase not only angered the board of regents but also taxed severely the already strained faculty resources of the university. So, accompanied by howls of protest from prospective students, the university reduced its enrollment for the fall of 1992 to the authorized level.

In the wake of that action came complaints from every category of student as well as from area legislators. The irony of the situation was not lost on faculty and staff who had seen the university through earlier periods of disappointing enrollments, identity crises, and lukewarm regional support.

Keeping the Faith

Through curriculum changes, administrative reorganization, underenrollments and overenrollments, and declining budgets, the question and concern commonly expressed has been, "Has the university maintained its identity and its special character and, if it has, can it continue to do so?" Every faculty and staff member who has participated in UWGB's evolution has an opinion on that matter.

Changes at UWGB over the first twenty-five years have been considerable. Gone are the Liberal Education Seminars. Gone are the theme colleges. Gone is most of the unusual nomenclature. Gone, too, is the ubiquitous environmental focus.

The 4-1-4 calendar with its January interim has survived, and the interim, among its other offerings, still contains opportunities for study abroad. But the calendar is under review by the Faculty Senate and the administration. The 4-1-4, a product of liberal arts colleges, has never been an easy fit at UWGB given its significant numbers of returning adult and part-time students. In recent years, enrollment pressures during the regular semesters have reduced availability of faculty to teach in January. In addition, a decline in interest among faculty in the interim has led to a downward spiral in January offerings and enrollments and once again has brought into question the efficacy of the 4-1-4 calendar at UWGB. The January interim may become the next component of the original academic plan to disappear as the institution continues to evolve.

But much of what the university is today remains closely tied to original concepts and aspirations. While the characterization of UWGB as "Eco-U" or "Environmental U" certainly has faded, bachelor's and master's degree programs, research, and outreach in such areas as environmental sciences and environmental policy and planning continue to be important components of the university, and interest in them is growing.

General education, guided by a faculty council and administered by a dean, continues to emphasize cross-cultural comparisons, as well as values or issues courses. All students participate in a capstone senior seminar before graduating. This seminar is a direct descendant of the Liberal Education Seminars.

The institution retains its long-time commitment to being student-oriented despite the challenges presented by burgeoning enrollments. Many small classes have become large classes, some project-oriented classes have disappeared, and some student services are overtaxed. But student-led courses remain, and a student can still design a personal major. The dean of students remains accessible. The library and computer center have enviable records of providing more with less. Academic advising is regularly judged an institutional strength.

Most significant, interdisciplinarity remains an integral part of the institution's character. Veteran faculty vigorously support the interdisciplinary approach, and new faculty are attracted to the university because of the possibilities it affords. Faculty organization remains focused on the interdisciplinary department. These departments support both the interdisciplinary and the disciplinary programs. The structure is the inverse of that found at most institutions, where disciplinary departments support the interdisciplinary programs.

Most students either major or minor in interdisciplinary programs, and these programs, far from disappearing, are some of the largest on campus. Even if the purists would argue that business administration must be excluded from the list, interdisciplinary programs in human development, humanistic studies, and environmental sciences are among the largest on campus. In addition, several programs not usually seen as interdisciplinary, such as social work, continue to be strongly influenced by the institutional commitment to interdisciplinarity. And a new interdisciplinary major in information and computing sciences was implemented in the mid-1980s.

Changes, of course, continue. At an institution still young, designed for flexibility, and under financial and enrollment pressures, change is not surprising. Some programs flourish, others are merged, redesigned, or dropped by the wayside. Demands for additional opportunities at the graduate level continue to increase.

UWGB, riding a crest of popularity, located in a growing region of the state, and already unable to adequately meet enrollment demands, faces a very different set of challenges in the 1990s from that faced during its early years. Like other public institutions in a university system, UWGB's success in meeting those challenges while maintaining a distinctive character will depend significantly on decisions outside its control.

EDWARD W. WEIDNER was founding chancellor of the University of Wisconsin-Green Bay. He is now chancellor emeritus and resides in Green Bay.

WILLIAM G. KUEPPER is vice chancellor for academic affairs at the University of Wisconsin-Green Bay.

Curricula at the University of California, Santa Cruz, combine universitywide courses offered by boards of studies with core courses, seminars, and other studies offered in each residential college.

University of California, Santa Cruz

Dean E. McHenry

Three decades after its conception, the University of California at Santa Cruz (UCSC) is still testing whether modest innovations launched at its birth can long endure. Some of the departures from the conventional appear firmly established, others have been modified, and still others have been long since abandoned. In baseball lingo, it appears that we have batted around .400 on the innovation front.

The University of California System

The University of California (UC) was launched in 1868 when the state merged the land grant idea and a classical private college. The flagship campus at Berkeley served a population of 500,000, but California grew so rapidly in numbers and complexity that additional campuses were established at Los Angeles, San Francisco, Davis, Santa Barbara, Riverside, San Diego, Irvine, and Santa Cruz.

During the 1950s, studies concluded that provision of higher education facilities was not keeping pace with the state's growth, which had a net increase averaging around 500,000 per postwar year. In 1957, the regents authorized three major new campuses, and Clark Kerr was chosen president of the university system (Stadtman, 1970).

An initial task was to organize the three segments of public higher education. This was accomplished by the formulation and adoption of the Master Plan for Higher Education (California State Department of Education, 1960). Adopted in 1960, it provided structure for postsecondary public segments: UC, state colleges (now the California State University System), and junior (now community) colleges. The master plan defined functions, curbed competition, provided for orderly growth, and recommended new campuses, including the three UC campuses added since 1960. The regents were able to obtain suitable sites for San Diego and Irvine at no cost to the university system.

Santa Cruz Is Born

After an extensive search for a site in northern California, the regents chose the Cowell Ranch, two thousand acres of forest and meadow, overlooking the small city of Santa Cruz and Monterey Bay. The Cowell Foundation, a charitable trust, sold the land at a nominal price with the understanding that it would contribute to improvements.

In 1961, I was appointed chancellor. Anticipating the choice of the rural and remote Santa Cruz site, Kerr and I had explored cluster college patterns. He called for diversity among the campuses (Kerr, 1963). We took a draft academic plan to the regents for provisional approval in 1962. It called for a federation of small liberal arts colleges, to be followed by graduate and professional schools. A team of architects prepared a physical plan during 1962–1963 (UCSC, 1963). Simultaneously, we refined the academic plan and commenced the search for leadership of the new enterprise (UCSC, 1965).

Residential Colleges. The main innovation of the Santa Cruz campus is its organization of the undergraduate sector into several residential colleges that combine the functions of an academic unit of administration with cocurricular aspects of student life. There was no single model for this undertaking, but precedents such as Oxford and Cambridge, Yale and Harvard, and Rice and the Claremont colleges were studied with care. And our admiration was great for the independent colleges that Kerr attended (Swarthmore) and at which he and I taught (Antioch and Williams, respectively). We also knew the excellent work done at Pomona and Occidental, Amherst and Wesleyan (Connecticut), Grinnell and Oberlin, and many others. But to our knowledge, no other large public U.S. university had attempted to organize its entire undergraduate establishment in this way.

We designed the residential college as the main focus of student and faculty identification and the principal instrument for achieving and retaining a sense of smallness. Colleges were to range in size from 250 to 1,000 students, with proportionate numbers of faculty fellows drawn from many fields of study. Each college is headed by a provost, a tenured faculty member, assisted by a small staff of preceptors. Courses were to be offered both by campuswide boards of studies in each of the major disciplines and by the colleges, mainly in interdisciplinary areas.

Physically, each college is a distinct entity, with classrooms, dining hall, and residential facilities for at least half of the undergraduate members and for supervisory personnel, including a house for the provost, small libraries, and modest recreational facilities. Colleges receive capital funds from three sources: the state (for educational facilities), revenue bonds (for student housing and feeding), and private gifts and grants (for other amenities).

Eight colleges were established in the first eight years: Cowell, Stevenson, Crown, Merrill, Porter, Kresge, Oakes, and Eight (still formally unnamed). Except for Stevenson and Eight, each was named for a foundation or family that provided private financing.

Campuswide Organization. Although most initial attention was given to the colleges, crucial (and conventional) decisions were also made concerning campuswide matters. First, the natural sciences were given their own laboratories, teaching space, and faculty offices outside of the colleges. This arrangement was deemed necessary in order to attract first-rate faculty members in the sciences. It raised the "two cultures" dilemma almost immediately. Many of the scientists, although fellows of their colleges, tended to visit them infrequently and to shun college assignments.

Recognizing the need for faculty members to keep up-to-date in their own disciplines, to plan majors and graduate work, and to participate in professional groups, national and regional, we saw the necessity of something like departments. But we tried to avoid some of the power-centered, exclusive, overspecialized attributes of departments. The critiques of conventional departments by Louis T. Benezet and Fred H. Herrington are convincing (McHenry and Associates, 1977). We tried to avoid some of the pitfalls by sharing decisions about new faculty members, and their advancement, with the provost of the college involved; using the name "board of studies" instead of department; and budgeting funds for faculty salaries through divisional deans and provosts. Soon after I retired in 1974, these safeguards, except for nomenclature, were modified. There were twenty-four boards in 1991.

Disciplinary groupings were headed by three deans of divisions. The divisional deanship was nothing new. Arts and sciences colleges within large universities commonly allocate departments among divisions or faculties. For several years (1967–1976) at Santa Cruz, we used the title vice chancellor, instead of dean, for heads of divisions. The original three divisions were humanities, social sciences, and natural sciences; in 1990, arts split off from humanities and became the fourth division.

In the first decade (1965–1975), campus growth consisted largely of undergraduate students accommodated in existing or new colleges. Modest growth took place during the next decade (1976–1986); no new colleges were organized and existing colleges were swamped with students, far beyond previously established levels. Rapid growth resumed in the late 1980s; among the new constructions were the large new colleges Nine and Ten, as well as three science buildings, one of which is a spectacular science library. Graduate enrollments grew slightly but, by 1992–1993, still constituted less than 10 percent of the total head count of students.

Ingredients for a Beginning

In planning UCSC, we faced a multitude of questions. For guidance on some of them, we could turn to institutions similar to what we were planning, but in many cases we had to fashion solutions of our own.

Gaining Support. In starting a new enterprise, particularly one with innovative approaches, planners must look for sources of support. The Santa Cruz experiment would not have been authorized without the strong backing of President Kerr. He persuaded the regents that the proposal was worth a try. Governor Edmund G. Brown made the crucial and bold decision to go forward with the three new UC campuses. The disorders on large campuses, particularly at Berkeley in the mid-1960s, persuaded legislators and others that new directions should be explored.

The 1960s were not an ideal time to start a new education institution, but when is? The groundwork was laid in the 1950s. Surveys showed that expansion of the UC System had not kept pace with the growth of the state. Serious problems needed to be worked out with other segments of higher education, which was eventually accomplished through the negotiation and approval of the master plan in 1960. The stage was set, all systems were "go."

In retrospect, it is hard to imagine when, if ever, a more favorable combination of leadership and conditions could be put together. Less than three decades after they were established, the three new campuses—Irvine, San Diego, and Santa Cruz—accommodated an aggregate of 40,000 students, who otherwise might not have found places in colleges or universities. Construction and operating costs then were relatively low, and the university system now has physical plants of great value and academic and supporting staffs that could not be replicated in any reasonable time.

The most essential part of capital costs came from the state's general obligation bond issues. The bond issue voted on in June 1962 was defeated just before I moved to Santa Cruz. The legislature put it on the ballot again in November and it carried, with Santa Cruz County giving the highest approval in the state. That was the first of several bond issue campaigns that we conducted under the slogan "Colleges for Tomorrow."

Publicity. From 1962 onward, leading newspapers and magazines covered the academic plan and praised it in editorials. The leading dailies of California and the New York Times carried numerous news stories. Time magazine saluted our "Oxford on the Pacific." Reader's Digest observed that our plan combined the advantages of the small college and the big university.

At one stage, we toyed with the notion of bringing famous people to the campus to catch the public eye and announce our existence in a dramatic way. We chose, instead, to gain recognition the traditional way, by awarding honorary degrees. The regents later decided to suspend awarding of honorary degrees, a blow to new, aspiring campuses.

Problem of Size. At the time that the three new campuses were endorsed in the master plan and given a "go ahead" by the state government, each was expected to top out at 27,500 students. Once the Santa Cruz site was chosen, I began to argue for a lower limit. The campus was distant from big metropolitan areas, thus precluding many commuters. Available studies of campus size indicated that a maximum of 10,000 to 15,000 would be desirable. Two universities that I admired, Stanford and Cornell, were in that range. It was 1989 before the regents finally accepted the limit of 15,000.

In the initial planning stage, we had to assume an ultimate total of 27,500 students, of whom perhaps 60 percent would be undergraduates in the arts and sciences. The number of residential colleges then was projected to be in the range of sixteen to twenty, with an average of 700 students per college. Moreover, new colleges were not organized between 1973 and 1991, which required the existing eight colleges to take heavy overloads.

Now that the regents have given final approval to the 15,000 maximum, planning can proceed with some assurance. Additional colleges are in the building program. It would appear that sixteen colleges, averaging around 775 each, can accommodate 12,500 undergraduates.

No one knows for certain the optimum size for a community or a campus, or a college. Different people, and different circumstances, call for different sizes. Our starting objective at Santa Cruz was to develop an environment in which a sense of belonging could prevail for gregarious students. Someone suggested a test: Student A meeting student B on a city street in Santa Cruz should be able to recognize him or her as a member of the same college. We hoped to reinforce acquaintanceships by such devices as having most students "live in," dine together, and take small classes within their own colleges. One of the great days for me came when a first-year student told me, "Five professors call me by name." For one brief, shining moment I thought that we had found a way to avoid impersonality as bigness overtook UCSC.

Student Evaluation. I, as the founding chancellor of UCSC, and the initial faculty of Cowell College were determined to make changes in the grading of students. We proposed to set aside the traditional letter-grade plan and replace it with pass/fail and narrative evaluation. The first-quarter letter grades were also recorded (but kept confidential) because permission for the change had to be obtained from the UCSC Academic Senate. Each narrative evaluation consists of a statement by the instructor about the nature of the course, an appraisal of the student's performance, and comments. Except for a few preprofessional courses, all students in all courses were graded by pass/fail and narrative. Later, the senate changed the procedure from pass/fail to pass/no report. In 1981, by a narrow vote, the senate adopted a proposal to allow students to request letter grades. The proportion of letter grades given remains under 10 percent.

The student evaluation issue is hotly contested. We who favored reform wanted to curb "grade grubbing" and rote memorization. We also maintained that a narrative, carefully written, can give a more adequate assessment of a student than can a grade point average. The cost of administering the narrative evaluations is high. Quann (1992) reported that UCSC processed thirty thousand narrative evaluations per term, at an added cost above a letter-grade plan of $304,000 per year. That cost figure does not take into account faculty time spent in writing the evaluations.

The range of evaluations of UCSC students includes "honors" and "highest honors" in the major; around 20 percent of B.A. and B.S. recipients are awarded one or the other. In addition, there are "college honors"; in a recent year, 11.4 percent of those graduating were so honored. The campus chapter of Phi Beta Kappa usually elects around 5 percent of graduating seniors to membership.

Course Offerings. Both Kerr and I called for limited course offerings, designed for student needs rather than faculty interests. Soon after the campus got under way, however, the number and variety of courses proliferated. Course approval is one of the matters wholly delegated to the academic senate, but its committees did not stem the tide. The volume of approved disciplinary courses was augmented by a large number of college courses. Initially, all courses had identical value: five quarter units. Over the years, however, courses of lesser credit were added for laboratory and similar work. The senate decision in 1991 to stimulate college course offerings encouraged approval of many one-, two-, and three-unit courses.

Campus Emphasis. Kerr and I also expressed an aspiration, early on, to emphasize social sciences and humanities at Santa Cruz. A good start was made; but after a quarter century of operation, the natural sciences appear to have achieved greater research distinction. The scientists have clearer standards for judging good work than do the rest of us. The campus boasts of thirteen members of the National Academy of Sciences on its active and retired roster. The largest number of them are in astronomy. We point with pride to the 1990 ratings of *Science Watch*, which placed UCSC first nationally in physical sciences and twelfth in biological sciences ("Small Can Be Beautiful Too . . . ," 1990). Small wonder that some wag called UCSC an institute of science and technology!

Class Size. One of the most deeply held aspirations of the fledgling Santa Cruz campus was to have close instruction in seminars and small classes. This goal had to be accomplished within the limits of a reasonable teaching load and the faculty-student ratio. Early on, we agreed the faculty should annually teach the equivalent of five courses of five quarter units. A somewhat richer faculty-student ratio was allowed in the formative years, but by 1973–1974 it had worsened to 1:18. The registrar's tabulation of enrollments in courses offered by boards of studies (excluding college and certain other courses) in two academic years is shown in Table 3.1. From these figures, it appears that a preponderance of small classes is still being achieved, despite reduced teaching loads, sabbatical leaves, and leaner faculty-student ratios. The increased number of teaching assistants has helped make possible the retention of a relatively favorable class-size pattern.

Architecture. The founding campus architect, John E. Wagstaff, and I

Table 3.1. Percentage Distribution of Class Sizes at the University of California, Santa Cruz, 1989–1991

Class Size	1989–1990	1990–1991
0–12	17.2	15.9
13–24	41.6	42.5
25–49	20.6	20.5
50–99	11.6	12.3
100–199	6.5	6.6
200+	2.6	2.3

shared many points of view on development of the campus. One was height of buildings. We had seen high-rise structures at the Berkeley, Los Angeles, and San Francisco campuses, each with annoyingly crowded elevators and the lessened sense of belonging. Given the collegiate plan and adequate land, we determined that, at least in the early years, we would risk the criticism of scatteration. In order to call attention to the decision, I began to use the expression "no building higher than two-thirds of a redwood tree." The idea came from H. Allen Smith's (1963) version of a Tahiti ordinance limiting the height of structures to two-thirds of a coconut tree.

The physical design of each college was assigned to different architectural firms. Diversity in designs was essential, each college as different from the others as are houses in a high-class residential district. The initial design and construction won considerable acclaim. Nearly all college complexes and core buildings won architectural awards. Biemiller's (1988) description of the architecture in the *Chronicle of Higher Education* pleased us immensely.

Unfortunately, however, when construction resumed in the second half of the 1980s, there were some mistaken sitings and less attractive designs. But the height limit has been maintained. By 1991, the physical planning process was back on track, and the next generation of building promises resumption of architectural distinction.

Cost Control. Aspects of the Santa Cruz plan alarmed some regents and some state officials. They assumed that our proposals would be too costly to adopt. More than once, Governor Brown greeted me by saying, "Santa Cruz is going to cost more, isn't it?" I maintained that we could and would raise funds for the extra capital costs from private sources, and that additional operating costs, if any, would be met without state funds—specifically, gifts and grants in the short run and income from college endowments in the long run. These endowments have been slow in coming; by 1992, the market values of some of the endowments were as follows: Porter, $2,843,000; Oakes, $1,061,000; Cowell, $323,000; Crown, $257,000; and Merrill, $185,000. In addition, unallocated college-endowed funds totaling over $300,000 are on hand. The unallocated sum includes $186,000 raised by "Pioneer classes" for Cowell and Stevenson.

Although these amounts appear substantial, they yield in interest far less than what is needed to adequately supplement meager state and student fee income. Obviously, the ultimate weapon to keep the colleges from overspending state and regental funds is to deny their requests at appropriation time.

Transportation. From the beginning, those of us who planned the campus sought to minimize the use of private automobiles. During the first five years, alternate forms of transportation were encouraged through mild pressures such as parking fees and few campus parking lots. Later, the students voted to vest student funds in a paved bicycle path running from the foot of the campus to the bottom of the campus core, and to assess themselves a modest quarterly charge (then $3.50 per student) to provide passes on the public bus system, usable for any route within Santa Cruz County. Both steps were initiated by students. By 1992, Metro buses connected downtown Santa Cruz and the campus eight times per hour during daytime. Both Metro and UCSC shuttle buses provide intracampus transportation. Bicyclists who find the hilly campus trying are offered free shower or bath facilities. Van pool arrangements are available for faculty and staff.

Courses Versus Units. In preparation for the opening of UCSC in 1965, several matters of policy could not wait for faculty deliberations. They ranged from high policy to mere housekeeping items. The UC System had already decided to shift the general campuses from the traditional semester plan to the quarter plan. The existing campuses were not scheduled to make this change until 1966; however, the three new campuses chose to commence with the quarter plan in 1965.

At Santa Cruz, we decided to go on a course rather than a unit basis. Our requirements were stated in terms of courses taken rather than units accumulated. The value of each course offered was equivalent to five quarter units. No courses of less than full value were contemplated—no one or two units for physical education or military training, as at other campuses. We argued that students should not have their attention spread over a flock of small courses, as high as six to eight in one term.

The line was held for several years. Then came the science course that needed a laboratory section, then the music practicum. Gradually, the campus returned to unit-based credits. The adoption by the senate of a report on the intellectual and cultural life of the colleges (see Academic Senate, 1991) has opened the floodgates, I fear, to a swarm of little courses and a return to a mechanical piling up of units from here and there to the total required for a degree.

Curriculum. Pending the arrival of substantial numbers of faculty, we proceeded to set up requirements for the bachelor's degree. They were the usual breadth requirements; each student must look into the sciences, humanities, and social sciences. We also required mathematics and ability to read, write, and speak a foreign language. Both have been modified, I regret to say.

"Lion Hunting" for Faculty and Staff

At the beginning of the search for academic leadership, I gave highest priority to finding senior scholars who had made marks in their own fields of study and who also had real interest in undergraduate education. It was of paramount importance that they be "true believers," convinced that the institution could be built with a balance between teaching, on the one hand, and research and creative activity, on the other.

Leadership. The first test of the plan's feasibility was the search for leading scholars to head the colleges. I scoured the university and college world. President Kerr was able to secure for the Santa Cruz and San Diego campuses the title of "provost" for the college heads. It was a happy choice. *Webster's* suggests several meanings of the term: "the chief dignitary of a collegiate or cathedral chapter," "the chief magistrate of a Scottish burgh," "a high-ranking university administrator." Page Smith (B.A., Dartmouth; Ph.D., Harvard), a distinguished historian from UC Los Angeles, was chosen to head Cowell. For Stevenson, we chose Charles Page (B.A., Illinois; Ph.D., Columbia), a sociologist from Princeton. Glenn Willson (B.A., Manchester; D.Phil., Oxford), a political scientist from Rhodesia and Nyasaland, took over Stevenson in 1967. Crown drew Kenneth Thimann (B.Sc. and Ph.D., Imperial College, London), one of the world's great biologists, from Harvard. Merrill attracted Philip Bell (B.A. and Ph.D., Princeton), an economist from Haverford. For Porter, we selected James Hall (B.A. and Ph.D., Iowa), a poet and writer from UC Irvine. For Kresge, we selected Robert Edgar (B.Sc., McGill; Ph.D., Rochester), a biologist from the California Institute of Technology. Herman Blake (B.A., NYU; Ph.D., Berkeley), a sociologist from UCSC, was chosen for Oakes. Stanley Cain (B.S., Butler; Ph.D., Chicago), a specialist in environmental studies from Michigan, was selected to chair Eight's planning committee.

In the 1960s, when UCSC opened, many institutions had mandatory retirement at age sixty-five. We availed ourselves of this opportunity to acquire senior leadership for a faculty heavily weighted on the youthful side. Our so-called Sixty-Five Club members included such stars as Robert D. Calkins, Lawrence R. Blinks, James Gilluly, Frederick Hard, Stanley Cain, Cornelis B. van Niel, and Bernard F. Haley. Although the ranks ultimately were decimated by re-retirement, the strategy is still viable in an era of early retirements.

The academic plan for UCSC mentioned the desirability of finding and recruiting qualified women. My own goal was to have women for one-third of the tenured and tenure track faculty. We made a good start in the 1960s and 1970s, but in the 1980s and early 1990s the supply of qualified women increased in sufficient numbers to make achievement of the hiring goal possible. As of fall 1991, women constituted 35 percent of the total faculty and 24 percent of the tenured faculty.

A similar hiring goal has stimulated searches for ethnic minorities. They are needed as role models for students of ethnic minorities and for ties to ethnic groups in California communities, as well as for their own promise and achievements as scholars and scientists.

According to UCSC's record of academic personnel, the campus has made a strong start in recruiting and maintaining a first-rate faculty. During the quarter century of operation, it has developed its own "lions" from cub status, including appropriate representation of women and minorities.

Administrators. On the general administration side, UCSC has less consistently scored well. Key early appointees performed with distinction. Among these were Francis H. Clauser, who served as vice chancellor; Harold A. Hyde, vice chancellor of business and finance; Gurden Mooser, assistant chancellor of university relations; Howard B. Shontz, assistant chancellor of student services and registrar; John E. Wagstaff, campus architect; and Donald T. Clark, university librarian. Clauser left to head engineering at the California Institute of Technology when our program was blocked. Hyde returned to private business in 1975. Mooser stayed on until 1978. Shontz returned to UC systemwide administration in 1973. Wagstaff resigned in 1974. Clark retired in 1973 but continues his scholarly work on local history.

In making faculty appointments, I often gave greater weight to undergraduate origins than to graduate school backgrounds. We sought faculty members who had experienced close instruction at top liberal arts colleges, such as Oberlin, Swarthmore, Amherst, Pomona, Occidental, Reed, and Carleton, or who had graduated from universities with carefully crafted undergraduate programs, such as Yale, Harvard, and the University of Chicago. Graduate degrees from the West and East coasts, especially those from UC Berkeley, Stanford, Harvard, Yale, Princeton, and Columbia, predominated in the initial faculty.

Looking back, I now think that the greatest personnel error of my administration was my failure to find and appoint as vice chancellor someone who was able and willing to take over when I retired. And I should have delegated more authority.

Students: The Best and Brightest

In developing plans for UCSC, we had to remind ourselves constantly that we would not be serving a typical student body, certainly not a representative sample of the American college student population. Although a public institution, UCSC would in many ways resemble a private university.

Scores and Honors. While planning the new campus, we had in mind a talented yet diverse lot of young people—the best and the brightest, of course, but with special qualities such as creativity and well-roundedness. The UC System determines the basic requirements for admission of undergraduate students in terms of high school coursework, academic record, and Scholastic Aptitude Test (SAT) scores. The Master Plan for Higher Education called for UC to draw its freshmen from the top 12.5 percent of high school graduates. At UCSC, we aimed toward even greater selectivity, drawing heavily from the top 5 or 6 percent. At the beginning, we had far more qualified applicants than we could accommodate, so we used the latitude to choose a remarkable initial student body. Surplus applicants were redirected to older UC campuses. At the height of its popularity, UCSC had four times the number of qualified applicants that could be accommodated.

During the 1960s, we were aware that we had an extraordinary group of students. This was confirmed by comparisons of the SAT scores of our freshmen with those of freshmen at other institutions. Average SAT scores for 1970–1971 (American Council on Education, 1973) showed that UCSC freshmen scored 1,257, combined verbal and mathematical, which was above the scores of other UC campuses. It also exceeded those of other state universities (followed by Virginia-Charlottesville arts and sciences, 1,206, and Michigan-Ann Arbor, 1,203). Among California liberal arts colleges, UCSC was between Occidental and Pomona in SAT scores.

UCSC's exalted standing in SAT scores did not last long. Relying on later American Council on Education (1983, 1987) data, we saw our students' average combined score drop to 1,071 in 1980, and to 1,083 in 1986, around midway among UC campuses and well below the scores of Virginia, Michigan, Pomona, and Occidental, with whom we once compared ourselves.

The honors won by our early graduates were astounding. In 1969, six won Woodrow Wilson Fellowships, proportionately the best in the California and Hawaii region. Two more won Danforth Fellowships, and one a Marshall scholarship to Great Britain. The number of awards declined in subsequent years but stabilized at a respectable level, well above national norms.

During the mid-1970s, the campus suffered several reverses. The Santa Cruz community was rocked by gruesome murders. Professional schools were deferred. Young people increasingly sought job-related training. Impersonality grew as the faculty-student ratio moved up to 1:18. The numbers of applications dropped, and the campus filled in vacant places with "redirects" from Berkeley and Davis. The gild was off the lily.

Underprivileged Students. We were determined to attract as high a proportion of economic and ethnic minority students as possible. The initial students were largely from middle-class and well-to-do families. Mexican Americans were particularly in need of support and encouragement. The campus provides special services to locate minority students of promise, to nurture their interest, and, when warranted, to waive admission requirements. Fortunately, a bequest of Alfred Hahn of close to $2 million provided an endowment to assist disadvantaged students. Ethnic minority students increased from 5 percent in 1968 to 15.2 percent in 1972. For 1991–1992, the figure was 26 percent.

Student Attitudes. President Kerr visited the new campus in 1965, during our first week of operation. "What are the students like?" he asked. I answered, "Mostly activist and intellectual. No Joe College types." He responded, "Then you're in for trouble." Student activism boiled over in the late 1960s and early 1970s. Passions were inflamed by the Vietnam War, the assassinations of the Reverend Martin Luther King and Senator Robert F. Kennedy, and riots in city ghettos. A regents meeting on campus was disrupted, as was the graduation ceremony for the first four-year class. Critics who accused us of creating an insulated haven to avoid activism found that just the opposite had happened.

Over the early years, we got an impression of how our freshmen differed from the national norm based on data from the annual surveys of freshmen conducted by the American Council of Education Office of Research. They tended to be younger, were more likely to have college-educated parents, and more often had high school grade averages of A+, A, or A−. They favored a deemphasis of college sports, rejected the notion that the benefit of college is monetary, and overwhelmingly favored preferential treatment of the disadvantaged.

These attitudes have changed little in successive waves of freshmen during the ensuing quarter century. "Big time" athletics were discouraged, but extramural teams, under National Collegiate Athletic Association (NCAA) Division III rules, competed, mainly with smaller institutions, and UCSC won national championships in tennis and fencing. So far "small is beautiful" has prevailed, but this philosophy is not without problems. Because physical education courses do not receive academic credit, state funds are not available for support. Expenses must be met from student fees, for which competition is intense. During 1991–1992, students who played on extramural teams (NCAA Division III) were required to pay $50 per sport, a far cry from the athletic scholarships that are available to subsidize athletes at many institutions.

As UCSC sports teams drew the attention of sports writers, an interesting contest ensued between Chancellor Robert L. Sinsheimer, who wanted "Sea Lions" as the teams' name, and students who preferred "Banana Slugs," slimy creatures of the redwood forest. After a protracted struggle, the Slugs won.

The founding fathers hoped that the small colleges, by providing small groupings, would make fraternities and sororities unnecessary. As the campus has grown and the colleges have reached overcapacity, however, some fraternal groups have been formed. Opponents are vocal, citing exclusiveness and loss of egalitarianism. The issue is far from settled.

Civic Spirit. All of my adult life I advocated a lowering of the legal age for voting. I argued that young people graduating from secondary school are ready to take on civic responsibilities. Since men are subject to military conscription at age eighteen, that seemed a logical age to start voting. To ease the impact, I suggested a gradual enfranchisement, spread over three or four years. The Twenty-Fifth Amendment to the U.S. Constitution, ratified in 1971, conferred the vote on all eighteen-year-old citizens.

Coupled with the liberalization of state laws on voter registration, this change in the voting age had a major impact on the politics of some communities in which colleges and universities are located. In Santa Cruz, new students arriving in late September could register and vote in the general election of November. Bona fide local residents have good cause to be alarmed that transient students have acquired the power to vote for locally elected officials and, especially, to vote on bond issues. The hurt is even greater when the institution that the students attend is exempt from local property taxes.

Student voting in local elections is one of the sore points in town-gown relations for UCSC. Some people in the community believe that the faculty indoctrinates students. Actually, students who choose Santa Cruz are, by and large, already "liberal." What alarms me is that many do not give both (or all) sides a fair hearing. In a typical general election, the campus precincts often poll 90 percent or more for so-called progressive candidates. Short of changes in federal and state voting laws, a more ideologically balanced student body at UCSC may depend on the addition of engineering and business programs.

Student Activities. Although the colleges were designed to be the main centers of students' extracurricular lives, some campuswide activities were inevitable. For example, considerations of space and money indicated that athletic and health facilities largely be centralized, some activities on a bicollege basis. In the beginning, intracollege activities such as music, drama, sports, yearbooks, newsletters, and interest groups abounded. Some still exist, but the centrifugal force increased as the campus grew larger and more specialized instruction became available.

Examples are numerous. Ethnic minorities band together in cross-campus organizations. Sports activities are centered in Physical Education and Recreation, with a minimum of competition between or among the colleges. College music groups are rare, as the Music Board sponsors most concerts. Productions of plays in the colleges have given way to performances sponsored by the Theater Arts Board. A central student union now competes with the colleges for social occasions and snack bar business.

The tide might be turned if the colleges were more energetic about fostering activity and interest groups. All could encourage foreign language tables at dinnertime. Provosts could encourage college athletic teams in intramural competition. There should be college-based debate teams and more public forums on current issues. Revival of college yearbooks would provide the colleges with records for identifying their own graduates for publicity and service to each college and the campus. Among the colleges' successful ventures are their coffee shops and snack bars, which are frequented by students and staff who live off campus. Some have become social institutions of note.

College Courses

To what extent should formal courses be offered in the colleges? This question was never fully settled, primarily because of diversity of opinion among faculty, students, and administrators.

College Core Courses. Beginning in 1965, the Cowell College core courses set a pattern that has been replicated, in different forms, by all of the subsequent colleges. At Cowell, a required course series for freshmen, called World Civilization, covered, in successive quarters, The Ancient World, The Medieval World, and Reformation to Present. There were three lectures per week, supplemented by seminars and tutorials led, with few exceptions, by regular faculty. The sophomore sequence of World Civilization included American Civilization; India, China, and Japan; and The Middle East.

Other colleges started broad core courses such as Culture and Society (Stevenson), Science, Philosophy, and Religion (Crown), and The Third World (Merrill). These orientation offerings were generally required of all first-year students and soon played a major role in helping the faculty fellows and students of each college to become acquainted. Each core course also provided an introduction to the college's theme.

Core courses have changed over the years, but they exist in all eight colleges. In most cases, there are lectures in plenary sessions and discussion sections. Few colleges now use regular faculty to teach the sections. Instead, they appoint teaching assistants and part-time instructors. All except one have a one-quarter core course; Stevenson has a three-quarter core course.

In the mid-1980s, the Academic Senate Committee on Educational Policy took a close look at core courses. It declared that these courses should, at the minimum, offer close teaching in small sections, careful and critical reading of texts, instruction on writing clear, well-organized prose, and instruction on how to participate in discussions "in a collegiate manner." The committee counted among other objectives such factors as students getting acquainted with faculty members, their exposure to a common cultural heritage, and sharing of a common learning experience. Main barriers to improvement of the usual lecture-cum-discussion section format were identified as cost and lack of interest by regular faculty members.

During 1992–1993, the core courses were as follows: Idea and Imagination in the Western Tradition at Cowell, Self and Society at Stevenson, World Culture at Crown, Social Change in the Third World at Merrill, The Heritage of Arts in a Multicultural Society at Porter, Cultural Intersections at Kresge, Values and Change in a Diverse Society at Oakes, and Global Transformations, Environment, and Community at Eight. Occasionally, one hears statements that such general education courses should be campuswide. I would argue against centralization. The core course is a key to college orientation of new students. Improvements should be sought to elevate, not diminish, the status of the colleges. Intercollege collaboration certainly is in order. To me, the core courses appear meagerly financed and involve too few senior faculty members. The core courses are perhaps the last best device to justify calling UCSC a collegiate university.

Other College Courses. Beyond the core courses, teaching by the colleges in the first decade led to a miscellaneous assortment of seminars, small and large classes, fieldwork, independent study, tutorials, and student-taught courses. The subject matter ranged from interdisciplinary topics related to the college theme to clearly disciplinary topics such as physics for nonmajors. Many courses addressed secondary interests of faculty fellows. Most, perhaps, were in response to pressure to do something for the college.

The college course situation prevailing in 1974–1975, after I retired, was chaotic. The number of courses offered by the colleges ranged from a high of eighty-three at Five (now Porter) to a low of twenty-eight at Eight. In addition to disciplinary majors offered by the boards of studies, the colleges offered the following: Western Civilization and Arts and Crafts and Their History (Cowell), Aesthetic Studies (Five, now Porter), Women's Studies (Kresge), Modern Society and Social Thought (Stevenson), and Latin American Studies (Merrill). Latin American Studies and Women's Studies have survived as campuswide majors; the others expired. From my perspective, the college course offerings of this period could have been classified into one or more of the following: (1) "pet" interests of faculty fellows and volunteers, (2) aspects of disciplines that boards were unready to offer, (3) watered-down disciplinary subjects to meet breadth requirements, or (4) a few large unstructured lecture courses popularly known as "Mickey Mousers."

If I were starting over again as chancellor, with the wisdom of hindsight, I would limit college offerings to the core courses and other interdisciplinary courses. My choice would be to have a battery of courses in each college, called simply freshman seminars and sophomore seminars. They would be taught by regular faculty fellows of each college. The instructor and topic of each section would be announced by each college to its own students and would be listed in the schedule of classes, but not in the catalogue. I would prefer to have the seminars carry full course credit (five quarter units), but lesser value could be assigned if faculty time could not be spared.

Intellectual and Cultural Life of the Colleges. During the last two decades, the role of the colleges has been studied repeatedly by administrators, the UCSC Academic Senate, and the student body. The only report on which positive action was taken was that of the Joint Subcommittee of the Committees on Educational Policy and Planning and Budget (Academic Senate, 1991). The subcommittee conducted a broad study, with submissions from a cross section of faculty members and others.

The recommendations, although cautious and mild, were opposed by a strong minority in a senate meeting and in a subsequent mail ballot. The report, presented in four motions, called for (1) approval in principle that colleges are "social and intellectual entities" with responsibilities to mount courses taught by senate (tenured or tenure track) faculty, to advise students, and to conduct extracurricular intellectual activities; (2) all faculty members to be fellows of colleges, with additional rewards for those who provide extraordinary service; (3) teaching of an additional one- to three-unit course every three years by senate members, or comparable service to undergraduate education, and stipends of ten-month salaries to be paid to fellows who agree to a two- to three-year term of college service; (4) continuation of the joint committee's work on refinement and implementation. All four motions were approved by the senate in plenary session and by mail ballot.

The first year after adoption of the report, little change was discernible. Porter lists in the 1992–1993 catalogue six new two-credit courses, none of which appears to be multidisciplinary. A budget crisis precluded salary augmentations. Preparation and processing of new courses takes time. Opposition to any strengthening of the colleges continues to be endemic. Meanwhile, students provide vocal support for the colleges, and alumni are beginning to provide financial support.

Undergraduate Research. The Santa Cruz campus has always maintained a graduation requirement of either a senior thesis or a comprehensive examination. Boards of studies vary widely in the way in which this mandate is met. Recently, around 25 to 30 percent of B.A. and B.S. degrees were completed with a senior thesis. I am particularly pleased when joint student and faculty research results in a published article. The proportion of graduating seniors writing theses fluctuated widely in the early years, ranging from a low of 9 percent in 1968–1969 (a year of intense activism) to 45 percent in 1971–1972.

Recapitulation

What, then, is the bottom line at UCSC? We have tried to build a different institution within the framework of the UC System. It started off in a flurry of excitement during a period of pessimism. We attracted remarkably able scholars and administrators. The early students broke records in scholastic attainment and honors. The residential colleges proved attractive to donors as well as students. Visitors were dazzled by the beauty of the site. Skilled architects won awards for their designs and praise for fitting buildings among the redwood trees. The narrative evaluation pleased most students tired of playing the "grade shark" game. At last, here were sports for recreation played by all, rather than by a few semiprofessionals.

This rosy picture is not widely held. The campus is not for everybody, only for the self-motivated. Student life is not as idyllic as described in the brochures. The "can do" attitude of early administrators began to be replaced by quotes from rule books. Young faculty members, once so anxious to spend time with students, found it advisable to get back to their research. The promised professional schools, engineering and business, met roadblocks. The expected cohorts of graduate students were slow to materialize.

Perhaps the greatest barrier to change was the "Berkeley image." The great and much-deserved reputation of UC Berkeley, paralleled by that of UC Los Angeles, caused most faculty members throughout the system to measure success in terms of research prestige and professional school reputations. And then there is the threat of the "weighted formula," under which for funding purposes a graduate student at dissertation level counts 3.5 and a freshman or sophomore counts 1.0. Devised over twenty years ago as a rough measure of the overall UC System work load, its application to budget allocations among campuses is bound to discriminate against a campus specializing in undergraduate education, such as Santa Cruz. The formula is stated in a current planning draft (Academic Senate, 1992).

UCSC has suffered from an imbalance in its student body and faculty. We are nearly all in the arts and sciences, almost none in agriculture, business, and engineering—which in other state universities afford variety in points of view. Finally, I feel constrained to comment in the delicate area of administrative stability: five chancellors have served since I retired in 1974.

References

Academic Senate. University of California, Santa Cruz (UCSC). *Intellectual and Cultural Life of the Colleges.* Santa Cruz: UCSC, 1991.

Academic Senate. University of California, Santa Cruz (UCSC). *Shaping Our Future.* Santa Cruz: UCSC, 1992.

American Council on Education. *American Universities and Colleges.* Washington, D.C.: American Council on Education, 1973, 1983, 1987.

Biemiller, L. "Spectacular Architecture at University of California at Santa Cruz: An Appreciation." *Chronicle of Higher Education,* Jan. 6, 1988.

California State Department of Education. *A Master Plan for Higher Education in California, 1960–1975.* Sacramento: California State Department of Education, 1960.

Kerr, C. *The Uses of the University.* Cambridge, Mass.: Harvard University Press, 1963.

McHenry, D. E., and Associates. *Academic Departments.* San Francisco: Jossey-Bass, 1977.

Quann, C. J. "Grading by Narrative Evaluation." Unpublished manuscript, University of California, Santa Cruz, 1992.

"Small Can Be Beautiful Too: UC Santa Cruz, University of Oregon Rank Among the Scientific Elite." *Science Watch,* 1990, *1* (10).

Smith, H. A. *Two-Thirds of a Coconut Tree.* Boston: Little, Brown, 1963.

Stadtman, V. A. *The University of California, 1868–1968.* New York: McGraw-Hill, 1970.

University of California, Santa Cruz (UCSC). *Long-Range Development Plan.* Santa Cruz: UCSC, 1963.

University of California, Santa Cruz (UCSC). *Academic Plan, 1965–1975.* Santa Cruz: UCSC, 1965.

DEAN E. MCHENRY *was founding chancellor of the University of California, Santa Cruz. He is now chancellor emeritus and resides in Santa Cruz.*

Through a combination of prior coursework, contract learning, credit for experience, standardized tests, and other methods of evaluating prior learning, this college without a campus provides adults an opportunity to complete requirements for undergraduate degrees.

Empire State College

James W. Hall, Richard F. Bonnabeau

Empire State College, a component of the State University of New York (SUNY), was founded in 1971, during the administration of Chancellor Ernest L. Boyer. Many of the elements that made the college innovative— faculty mentorship, individualized learning contracts, assessment of nonformal experiential learning, field study, and distance education— existed elsewhere in American higher education. Empire State College's principal and unique contribution to nontraditional education has been the creation of a mentor-based approach to student academic planning and evaluation and an administrative ability to bring precisely the necessary academic resources from the multicampus SUNY System or from the community to the service of a single student's education needs. For the first time, on a statewide basis, off-campus students were offered a wide range of education options to individually tailor their academic studies (Hall, 1991, p. 93). Since the founding of Empire State College, which offers associate, baccalaureate, and master's degrees, over twenty thousand students have graduated. There are now more than forty regional learning locations throughout New York State, both in urban and rural locations, as well as abroad in Israel and Cyprus.

Breaking New Ground: Structure and Pedagogy

Consensus on the policies and practices that would govern the college was reached quickly in what can be best described as a rapid-fire planning process. Boyer established a planning task force in late October 1970, and by the end of January 1971 he had a resolution from the SUNY Board of Trustees to create Empire State College. The first students enrolled in September of

NEW DIRECTIONS FOR HIGHER EDUCATION, no. 82, Summer 1993   © Jossey-Bass Publishers

that year. Boyer's task force, composed of his top staff, did not have a preestablished notion of what SUNY's nontraditional program or college would look like. They were told to wipe academic history away and to plan without regard to traditional academic concerns (Dodge, 1991, p. 7). They briefly toyed with the British Open University (BOU) model of tutorials-in-print courses, paced by British Broadcasting Corporation's television and radio programs. BOU was a few months from enrolling its first students, however, and still untried. Under Chancellor Samuel B. Gould, SUNY had experimented with the State University of the Air program—SUNY's version of the BOU—but many years and millions of dollars later, the program had failed to attract students.

The failure of SUNY of the Air made it easy to bypass its more sophisticated British incarnation, originally called University of the Air, in favor of a flexible mentor-based model proposed by James W. Hall, assistant vice chancellor for policy and planning. This model, subsequently embellished by Boyer's task force, freed students from the curriculum straitjackets of SUNY of the Air and BOU. The mentor-based model incorporated the best elements of programs found at colleges such as Goddard and Antioch as well as technology-based education developed by SUNY and other institutions. The engine of this innovative academic machine, however, was the tailoring of programs to individual students, and the permutations of these programs were potentially infinite. Consequently, the institutional structure of the new college had to be embedded in a student-centered pedagogy.

Boyer's task force recognized that the survival and development of Empire State College depended on a clearly and forcefully articulated mission. By February 1971, the task force had prepared a prospectus for the college. *Prospectus for a New University College: Objectives, Process, Structure, and Establishment* (State University of New York, 1971) became the expression of values for Empire State College. The prospectus proclaimed the sovereignty of the individual student in the dawn of a new age for public higher education. No subsequent publication of note, in the early history of the institution, failed to mention its guiding force.

The prospectus called for the college to serve a "variety of individuals of all ages, throughout the society, according to their own life styles and educational needs." The college would rely on a process, rather than a structure, of education to shape and give it substance as well as purpose. It would seek to transcend conventional academic structures, which impose required courses, set periods of time, and residential constraints on individual students. The major focus would be the student and the process of learning. Master teachers would provide counseling and guidance to help students design programs of study to meet their individual education objectives, fully taking into account their current educational experience. This process would place responsibility for learning on the students in return for their freedom to pursue their educations according to individual needs and interests (State University of New York, 1971, pp. 4–19). More than two decades later these same principles hold fast.

An Independent College

One of the task force's critical recommendations was to create a freestanding institution. This independence explains why Empire State College has survived and flourished, even, at times, in the face of fiscal hardship. At first, the task force considered a program structurally integrated with the rest of SUNY, consisting of service centers located on campuses across the state. Credits earned would be easily transferable from campus to campus or to a central credit bank and thus applicable to a universitywide degree (Ertell, 1970). After further deliberation, the task force wisely recommended that Boyer ask the SUNY Board of Trustees to create a new college rather than propose yet another program coordinated by the SUNY System office. The task force did not have to search far to appreciate the wisdom of this course of action. SUNY of the Air, a statewide program not authorized to grant degrees, was administered by the SUNY System office. The program depended on, and failed to sustain, campus-based support. With the departure of Chancellor Gould and the advent of bad fiscal times, it became moribund. In part, Empire State College rose phoenixlike from its ashes, when SUNY transferred a good portion of this nontraditional program's budget and some of its talented personnel to the new college.

Boyer championed the recommendation to create an independent college. For him, the independence of the college—free of the control of one of SUNY's existing campuses and free of the chancellor—was an absolute requirement (Boyer, 1990, p. 4). Without this independence, according to Boyer, Empire would be "the chancellor's college." The new college should not only have its own president, council, and faculty but also its own administrative site, despite the fact that it is a noncampus (Boyer, 1990, p. 13).

External Funding: Carnegie and Ford

To ensure the SUNY Board of Trustees' support for a new independent college, especially at a time when SUNY's revenues were shrinking, Boyer moved swiftly to capture funding from the Carnegie Corporation and the Ford Foundation, and he succeeded in landing major grants, $500,000 from each. The much-publicized grants placed the enterprise in the national spotlight. Additionally, Boyer adroitly used the launching of BOU to strengthen his call for a SUNY nonresidential college. A team of his top staff, headed by Deputy Vice Chancellor Ertell, went to England. Although, as Lord Perry, BOU's first vice chancellor, later expressed, Empire State College and BOU were "as different as chalk and cheese," Ertell reported to the board of trustees that there was a huge demand for nontraditional education (SUNY Board of Trustees, 1970, pp. 8–9).

To further strengthen his position with the board of trustees, Boyer sought and received strong support from Governor Nelson A. Rockefeller, who took to the proposal with enthusiasm (Boyer, 1990, p. 5). Boyer was able, then, to go to the SUNY Board of Trustees on January 27, 1971, and request a resolution for a nonresidential, degree-granting college. The board unanimously supported the resolution for an independent college with the mission of drawing on the resources of the entire SUNY System to devise new patterns of independent study and flexible approaches to learning and thereby providing accessibility to young people and adults for whom off-campus individualized instruction is most effective (SUNY Board of Trustees, 1971, pp. 11–12). By fall 1971, Harry Van Arsdale, Jr., a powerful and highly respected New York City labor leader, lent his support to the enterprise when Boyer, with Governor Rockefeller's urging, agreed to have Empire State College create the nation's first accredited college program in industrial and labor relations for trade union membership (Rosenberg, 1989, pp. 56–114).

Institutional Framework: Process and Access

The emphasis in the board of trustees' resolution on use of the resources of the entire university system was a critical point. Up to that point in time, SUNY had been engaged in a period of frenzied growth as it responded to baby boomers who had reached college age and to the massive pressures on college admissions caused by the Vietnam War. Another bond issue to build yet another SUNY campus was out of the question. What seemed called for was a college that was built without bricks and mortar and that received its substance and purpose from "a process, rather than a structure, of education" (State University of New York, 1971, p. 4). This process could harness the prodigious resources of the SUNY System and communities throughout New York State to serve individual students.

For the first time, a public college, intended to serve large numbers of students, would design its program to respond to individuals personally. The institutional framework of the new college had to reflect process and pedagogy. Rather than have the student come to the college, the college would go to the student. It did so in a vigorous and bold way. Hall, whom Boyer appointed to get the college off and running, quickly broke away from the notion that centers should be limited to SUNY campuses: "The success of Empire State College is not based upon the reliability of construction schedules or the ability of the bond market to support ever higher levels of building. Empire State will require relatively modest quarters throughout the state, and will utilize existing structures (shopping centers, church education buildings, schools, public buildings, existing University facilities) in establishing its Learning Access Centers. This eliminates delays in program development, and places emphasis squarely on the educational objectives of the College" (Hall, 1971, p. 11).

In the first year of operation, Hall worked very hard and fast to extend Empire State College statewide before anybody could balkanize the college through regional limitations (Hall, 1990b, p. 8). Regional learning locations, each staffed by a critical mass of faculty representing a wide range of academic interests and working in the absence of a departmental structure, were established in New York City, Long Island, Westchester and Rockland, Albany, Rochester, and Buffalo. Additionally, these locations spawned outreach units, staffed by one or two faculty, to serve rural populations in situ or to offer specialized programs. In each instance, the regional learning locations were administered by a dean and an associate dean. Each had a large degree of regional responsibility but was responsive to a core administration in Saratoga Springs.

Size was a critical factor as well. The regional learning locations were small enough so that administrators and faculty worked as teams, not in opposition. They would all know each other and they would know all of the students on a personal basis. In effect, this size limitation created a series of organizational modules that fit together into what was actually a large statewide organization but one that operated with a tremendous amount of individual involvement (Hall, 1990a, p. 22). Although the regional learning locations exercised a good deal of local initiative, the kind that allowed them to be responsive to their communities, Hall and his associates recognized the importance of creating a reasonable consistency and similarity among them in the quality and nature of the products (Chickering, 1990, p. 44). It was important, therefore, to recruit faculty and deans who were committed to the basic education principles of the college (Chickering, 1990, p. 44). Other measures that promoted the development of a unified college culture over the years included a strong system of governance, regular gatherings of faculty and administrators, collegewide faculty and professional staff development activities, and a sophisticated computer-based communications system. The college is remarkable for having a faculty and professional staff, though in many instances separated by hundreds of miles, enjoying close and highly productive working relationships.

More than two decades later, the college holds fast to the principle of providing access, though hefty cuts in state funding have required some streamlining. The number of locations, which were rapidly established throughout the state in the first years, has grown steadily. The most recent addition is the New York Telephone Corporate/College in New York City. Headquartered at New York Telephone Computer Technology Learning Center in Manhattan, the program serves employees at New York Telephone sites in Manhattan, Brooklyn, Queens, and the Bronx. Additionally, the Center for Distance Learning serves students, including handicapped students, who are unable to meet face to face with their mentors. These include students who have been transferred from jobs in New York State to such places as Saudi Arabia, South Korea, Japan, and the Netherlands. The college, then, has reached a point in its evolution where it has the ability to serve students "according to their desires, interests and capacities" (State University of New York, 1971, p. 4) virtually anywhere in the world where telephone, mail, fax and, increasingly, computers ensure good communication between the student and the mentor.

A New Faculty Role

The task of bringing the college to the students and fulfilling their interests with sound programs of study required that the students be treated as individuals and not batch processed. To achieve this goal, a path-breaking faculty role was created. The term *mentor*, first applied by Hall, defined a new breed and a new use of faculty. Initially, the lack of a clear definition of the mentor role in the prospectus created a tendency among administrators to want to invite people who were primarily counselors to become mentors. But Hall resisted this approach. He wanted faculty to put the students at the center, but the faculty also had to know something (Hall, 1990a, p. 21). This initial confusion about the role originated in the thinking of the late 1960s about teachers as facilitators, advisers, and counselors. Hall and his associates decided not to hire people with degrees in counseling; instead, they sought people who had a counselor's perspective and skills but who were also very strong in a broad area of subject matter (Chickering, 1990, p. 17). Hall and Arthur Chickering, the founding academic vice president, wanted to create a relatively egalitarian faculty role—egalitarian in that two individuals, the faculty member and the student, were coming together to create a series of learning experiences. They recognized that the faculty member had to be knowledgeable, capable of serving as a resource person, and in command of broad-based expertise—because he or she would be dealing with a wide range of students—rather than great depth in a narrowly defined area. They wanted people who were good listeners, skillful in helping people clarify the purposes of their degree programs and their learning contracts, and who would not have prepackaged sets of objectives or assumptions to impose on students. In short, mentors had to be able to respond flexibly to students from very diverse backgrounds (Chickering, 1990, p. 16).

Time has tested the wisdom of this decision. Mentors with diverse academic interests continue to provide high-quality advising in degree program planning. Additionally, they serve as tutors to their own as well as other mentors' students and also pursue related scholarly interests. In this way, the college has continued to preserve and nurture its academic program. Of course, mentoring is a demanding, sometimes exhausting, role. This is a result of the great diversity of students, the clerical and supervisory dimensions of mentoring, the constant need to locate and train tutors, and the demands of local and collegewide committee service. Mentors who also coordinate outreach units face additional challenges. While coordinators are in almost no respect absolutely different from their colleagues, the needs for academic breadth, organizational management, community relations, and supervision are significantly greater (Empire State College, 1989, p. 29).

The issue of work load intensity has been echoed in various college reports throughout the years, including the most recent self-study for accreditation. While the college continues to move diligently toward making the faculty workload more manageable by reducing the full-time equivalence targets, by providing support materials and alternatives, and by easing the clerical and procedural dimensions of the role, the complexity or fragmented nature of the workload remains essentially the same. It is at the very heart of the college.

The mentor role has remained constant because the fundamental purpose of the college has remained unchanged. The college exists to fulfill the "individual needs and objectives of the student" (State University of New York, 1971, p. 15). It is the mentor, through the vehicle of learning contracts negotiated with the student, who marshals the rich and complex resources of communities, including the faculty of local colleges, to bring the student's degree program to fruition. A traditional college might have difficulty in meeting the needs and objectives of a single student, even if lecturing were the student's preferred mode of learning. The goal of meeting the needs of hundreds or thousands of students would be an impossibility were a college not to seek alternatives to the professorial model. BOU brought the classroom to the student in ingenious ways, but course teams defined the purpose, content, and the trajectory of learning. The student's individual needs and objectives had to remain subordinate because the university was the sole provider of learning resources.

Forging a Student-Centered Pedagogy

In having students define their own curricula, Empire State College had to open up an entire universe of learning resources. For Hall and his associates, this presented a serious challenge. Primarily, students could not just willy-nilly go off to study. They needed guidance and they needed their progress recorded. The learning contract, which had progenitors at Goddard and Sarah Lawrence, provided the solution, and the term *learning contract* was much more appealing than the amorphous phrase *independent study*. The learning contract offered something tougher, more rigorous, and more in the nature of a binding agreement between the institution and the individual because these qualities defined the essence of the education program at

Empire and the basis of the individual's enrollment. So, in the language of the contracts between the institution and the individual students, there is reciprocity and a mutual focus on learning (Chickering, 1990, p. 13).

Moreover, the learning contract provided an organizing structure for marshaling resources within the community—academic, social, governmental, and cultural (Dodge, 1991, pp. 15–16). Negotiated with the mentor and reviewed by colleagues, the contract defined the student's objectives, the content of learning, the modes and criteria of evaluation, and the amount of credit. Further, the contract reflected the mentor's and, ultimately, the college's judgment about the student's ability to undertake the study and its appropriateness as a subject of academic inquiry. Contracts in the early years of the college were elaborate documents. While they were remarkable for detailing the richness of the student's plan of study, mentors, for years, groaned under their weight. The college, therefore, moved toward streamlined documents. Today, the emphasis is on evaluation. The primacy of the learning contract as the academic coin of the realm remains unassailed, however.

In preparing the prospectus, the SUNY task force anticipated that the college would serve a wide variety of students with diverse needs and recognized the appropriateness of accommodating a wide spectrum of alternative education programs: "It will provide the resources both for structure, if necessary, and for individual creative learning" (State University of New York, 1971, p. 6). Hall thus believed that the depth and complexity of the college mission required different viewpoints to be brought together into one institution—for the benefit of the students—so that Empire would not be a single-mode institution (Hall, 1990b, pp. 10–11). With this in mind, Hall recruited Arthur Chickering as vice president for academic affairs and Loren Baritz as provost for instructional resources.

Chickering had been at Goddard during the 1960s and his book *Education and Identity* (Chickering, 1969) had won the National Book Award from the American Council on Education. Chickering liked what he saw in the prospectus. Many of the principles were entirely consistent with his experiences at Goddard and with the Union for Experimenting Colleges and Universities, as well as voiced by his contacts at both Antioch and Monteith. Loren Baritz, a respected colleague of Hall in the SUNY-Albany history department and a popular teacher who used multimedia presentations to enrich his classes, was aware of a kind of deadness that had developed. Baritz was interested in an approach to the undergraduate curriculum that would motivate students to learn more dynamically. He was interested in brilliant teaching, using every means at hand. And he saw at Empire State College, and also in the media of print materials and so on, a way to create something more dynamic in the curriculum, namely, innovative modules for structured, independent study (Hall, 1990b, pp. 10–11).

Although they differed strongly in their viewpoints, Baritz and Chickering shared powerful ideas about what was in need of change in higher education (Hall, 1990b, p. 10). Their differences created a wide spectrum in which Empire State College's mission would flourish, but not without the heated debates that accompany strongly held views. For Chickering, Empire State College had the potential to be a more refined version of Goddard. Chickering viewed the prospectus as an invitation to devise an individualized curriculum for each student through contract learning. He did not want a preestablished curriculum, believing that once a curriculum, no matter how creative, is defined, it becomes the driving force and the individual must be subordinate to it. Chickering's approach of designing individualized curricula was truly revolutionary (Hall, 1990b, pp. 11–12). To Baritz, the strategy of responding to students as individuals did not mean going beyond the meeting of their intellectual needs, nor did it mean constructing individualized curricula (Hall, 1990b, p. 13). Although he shared with Chickering the mission of creating student-centered alternatives to traditional education, Baritz had doubts about the readiness of all students to pursue individualized study. Disagreeing with Chickering over the idea that every curriculum had to be individually constructed through a contract with an individual student, Baritz chose structured independent study through the development of high-quality print-based modules, designed by scholars of national renown (Hall, 1990b, pp. 10–11).

Today, the range of students' options flowing from the differences between Chickering and Baritz has been preserved. One approach did not vanquish the other. Both survive, indeed flourish, because the individual needs of students determine the mix. The learning spectrum remains very broad. At one end, there is the Harry Van Arsdale, Jr., School of Labor Studies, which provides classroom instruction; the long-established practice of student cross-registration in SUNY campuses and other colleges; and guided independent study courses offered by the Center for Distance Learning. At the other end, there are completely individualized contract learning and degree programs. In between is an array of approaches that fulfill student-centered needs (Empire State College, 1989, p. 45). The preservation of this broad spectrum has sustained the flexibility and vitality of the college.

Validating Prior Learning

As mentioned earlier, another major principle articulated in the prospectus was the necessity of fully taking into account the student's current educational experience when designing a program of study. If the college was to take seriously the mission of fulfilling individual education objectives, it had to examine closely each student's academic history, both formal and experiential. Education objectives reflect equally the student's past as well as aspirations for professional competence and intellectual growth. This is especially so for adult students, who bring with them not only prior college study but often prodigious amounts of sophisticated learning from other arenas of their lives, such as employment and cultural interests. Much of this learning, because of its individual nature, is beyond the reach of standardized testing. Hall and his associates wanted to recognize these accomplishments. They reasoned that if students can learn informally, under the aegis of a university outside of the classroom, they can learn informally without the university outside of the classroom (Dodge, 1991, p. 10). Both Goddard and Antioch students, for decades, had amply demonstrated the former in every conceivable theater of learning.

As in other matters, the SUNY task force established the policy of recognizing prior learning but left the task of how this would work in practical terms to others. A simple but highly effective system of evaluation evolved through trial and error in Empire's early years and became a national model. The assessment of informal experiential learning and other forms of advanced standing were made part of the process of individual degree program planning. A degree program consists of prior learning and contractual learning presented in a single format, showing integration and progression in the concentration and in general learning. Expert evaluators assess the student's experiential learning, and the mentor submits the evaluations, the supporting documentation, including transcripts when applicable, and a student rationale essay to a faculty assessment committee.

Over the years, this practice has been highly successful, but it was a labor-intensive activity for mentors. To ease the burden, center assessment professionals assumed more of the task of attending to the prior learning components of degree programs. Additionally, to diminish the frustration expressed by students with regard to the length of the assessment process, which has a bearing on attrition, students are now informed much earlier about the amount of transcript credit available for degree program planning. Moreover, students are encouraged to undertake degree program planning as soon as it is appropriate. In some instances, degree programs are "approved" at centers prior to formal evaluations of the students' prior learning. Other measures are now under consideration to streamline the assessment process and to make it more responsive to student needs and less burdensome for faculty.

Overall, the essential policies governing the practices of degree program planning have remained unchanged: Faculty work closely with students in degree program planning; the degree program reflects the education objectives of the student, as weighed in the context of curriculum guidelines developed by the faculty for the eleven broad areas of study offered by the college; standardized tests and expert evaluators are employed to assess experiential learning; faculty committees review and approve degree programs and portfolios; there are consistency and fairness in assessment practices throughout the college; and final review and approval is certified by the Office of Academic Affairs. Although credit awards vary from individual to individual, current practice reveals that a substantial amount of advanced standing is recognized. The average student receives seventy-four credits, of which forty-seven are for previous college work and twenty-seven are for nonformal learning. Most important, a founding principle of the college, the commitment to validate what adult students already know, remains as fresh, poignant, and educationally significant as it was twenty-one years ago.

Conclusion

The success of Empire State College is best explained by the institution's enduring commitment to the principles articulated in the SUNY task force prospectus. The prospectus gave the college a strong sense of mission and values, on the basis of which the institution accommodates a broad spectrum of alternative educational programs for a remarkably diverse student clientele. While the prospectus clearly defined the principles that guided development of the college, the task force left the forging of policies and practices to others. The founding administrators and faculty came to Empire State College with a strong sense of mission, shared beliefs about the social importance of the institution, and commitment to its new pedagogies. The creation of a student-centered college, designed to fulfill a wide range of educational needs while preserving academic rigor, called for unbridled imagination, sober pragmatism, and a degree of fearlessness.

The college benefited enormously by not being overly planned by Boyer's task force. The most important decision in creating Empire State College was to begin immediately with students and faculty. In this way, policies and practices emerged from direct interaction with students. At one level, this approach was an expression of the fundamental philosophy of Empire State College, to pay attention to the students and to be responsive to them, but it was also, programmatically, a wonderful way to create a new institution (Chickering, 1990, p. 20). In the 1960s, a number of innovative colleges were undermined by long and laborious planning and became locked into new rigidities and other orthodoxies.

As an autonomous component of SUNY, the college is free to experiment. In the early years, the college devised policies and practices governing admissions, creation of a new faculty role, contract learning, degree program planning, assessment of informal experiential learning, linkages with other SUNY campuses and the resources of local communities, development and dissemination of independent study materials, creation of learning locations, and outreach to students with a variety of needs and backgrounds. In effect, the independent college was free to make critical and, in hindsight, productive choices about its fundamental nature and organization. Over the years, Empire State College has refined its policies and practices, but the college is essentially the same institution it was in 1974 when it received the first public nontraditional regional accreditation.

Empire State College, in redefining the education options of adult learners, brought to public higher education the kind of personal, interactive, nurturing experience once thought possible only in small residential, usually church-related, liberal arts colleges. In time, this may come to be Empire State College's most enduring achievement.

References

Boyer, E. L. "Empire State College Oral History Project." Empire State College Archives, Saratoga Springs, New York, Aug. 31, 1990.

Chickering, A. W. *Education and Identity*. San Francisco: Jossey-Bass, 1969.

Chickering, A. W. "Empire State College Oral History Project." Empire State College Archives, Saratoga Springs, New York, Aug. 16, 1990.

Dodge, W. R. "Empire State College Oral History Project." Empire State College Archives, Saratoga Springs, New York, Feb. 26, 1991.

Empire State College. *Retrospect and Prospect: Strengthening Learning at Empire State College*. Saratoga Springs, N.Y.: Empire State College, 1989.

Ertell, M. "Memorandum to Ernest L. Boyer." Empire State College Archives, Saratoga Springs, New York, Nov. 4, 1970.

Hall, J. W. "Memorandum to Ernest L. Boyer." Empire State College Archives, Saratoga Springs, New York, July 6, 1971.

Hall, J. W. "Empire State College Oral History Project." Empire State College Archives, Saratoga Springs, New York, Mar. 16, 1990a.

Hall, J. W. "Empire State College Oral History Project." Empire State College Archives, Saratoga Springs, New York, June 13, 1990b.

Hall, J. W. *Access Through Innovation: New Colleges for New Students*. New York: Macmillan, 1991.

Rosenberg, B. "An Examination of the Development of the First Accredited Labor College in the United States." Unpublished doctoral dissertation, Rutgers University, 1989.

State University of New York. *Prospectus for a New University College: Objectives, Process, Structure, and Establishment*. Albany: State University of New York, 1971.

State University of New York (SUNY) Board of Trustees. "Minutes." Empire State College Archives, Saratoga Springs, New York, Dec. 16, 1970.

State University of New York (SUNY) Board of Trustees. "Minutes." Empire State College Archives, Saratoga Springs, New York, Jan. 27, 1971.

JAMES W. HALL is the founding and current president of the State University of New York Empire State College, Saratoga Springs.

RICHARD F. BONNABEAU is a mentor and serves as the institution historian and archivist at Empire State College.

Organized on the cluster college concept, the University of West Florida promises an education comparable to the best of the small private colleges while making available to the student the kinds of resources that only a university can offer.

University of West Florida

Alfred B. Chaet

The opening of the University of West Florida (UWF) in 1967 was as welcome as the sun rising over the Gulf of Mexico. At the time, the panhandle of Florida was a relatively underdeveloped and unsophisticated section of the state, but it had great growth potential, since much of the rest of the state was already heavily developed. Encouraged by a number of determined and prominent Pensacolians, the West Florida legislative delegation argued that Pensacola was an ideal site for a new state university, not only because of existing needs in the area but also because of anticipated growth and development. The state legislature enacted enabling legislation and appropriated funds to establish the university in 1963. The first president, Harold Crosby, was appointed in 1964, and the new university began.

Late-Night Thunder

Controversy developed as soon as the legislators discussed the possibility of a new university in Pensacola. The local junior college, a strong institution, had aspirations to become a four-year university and was threatened by the prospect of an upper-level institution virtually next door, but after a great deal of bitter wrangling, a new freestanding, upper-level university was authorized.

The establishment of upper-level universities was a natural concomitant of the existing plan to develop junior colleges within reasonable commuting

The author expresses his appreciation to Arthur H. Doerr, Boland Professor of Environmental Studies and professor emeritus at the University of West Florida, for his advice on this chapter.

distance of all Florida citizens. UWF and its administration attempted to learn from its Florida predecessor, Florida Atlantic University, and from other upper-level universities across the United States.

Planning Without Committees

The administrative plan for this innovative university was developed with only a handful of administrators, before any faculty had arrived. The blueprint was conceived principally by its first president, but contributions were made by a few administrators appointed one to two years before the first students matriculated. The design included principles and policies already in effect at other innovative universities, but the planners deliberately omitted elements antagonistic to the education of students. Rarely does a fresh, innovative, and workable approach to education survive presentation to a committee of educators; typically, the plan becomes watered down and unrecognizable during negotiations. Without the presence of faculty, hence without the impediments of academic bickering and scholarly territoriality, a small number of academic administrators facilitated the development of innovative plans for UWF. In a real sense, the institution was the visible manifestation of the president's dream, modified only to a limited degree by administrative advisers.

Thus, the basic philosophy and structure of the university was inscribed in wet concrete, and only details remained to be added. This plan worked surprisingly well for the first ten years of operations, gave UWF considerable positive exposure, and permitted the development of patterns different from those of conventional institutions.

Storm Clouds

The plan was finalized in spite of major disagreements expressed by three or four top academic administrators who had already been hired (deans or associate deans for arts and sciences, business, and education). The disagreements revolved around whether to develop a traditional college structure or to initiate a cluster college approach. The cluster college concept represented a serious departure from the conventional university structure and was a threat to those whose prior academic experience was limited to the "College of . . . " framework. Other planners thought that it would be a great educational experiment to avoid the pitfalls and limits of this traditional framework. After the president considered all of the input, the cluster (originally referred to as "residential") college concept prevailed, and three independent, self-contained colleges (Alpha, Gamma, and Omega), each consisting of a mix of diverse disciplines, were established. Each college was assigned at least one department from the business, education, humanities, science, and social science disciplines. The initial academic groupings are shown in Table 5.1.

Table 5.1. Initial Assignments of Departments to
Residential Colleges, University of West Florida

Discipline Area	Alpha College	Gamma College	Omega College
Business	Marketing	Finance Accounting	Economics Management
Education	Professional Education	Elementary Education Physical, Health, and Recreation Education	Vocational- Technical Education
Humanities	English Foreign Languages Communication Arts	Philosophy Religion Music	Art
Science	Mathematics Statistics	Biology Chemistry	Physics
Social Science	Psychology Sociology Anthropology	History	Political Science

Although each dean was assured a pivotal position under the new plan, several of the initial appointees said that they could not function under a plan that did not recognize separate units for education, business, and arts and sciences. They resigned and departed before the first students set foot on campus in 1967. In spite of some discontent among faculty, students, and administrators, the cluster college plan, established in the absence of academic committee structure, persisted for a decade. The advantages of this bold structure outweighed the disadvantages.

Upper-Level University

Since the university was an upper-level (junior and senior) and graduate (master's) institution, it depended heavily on the junior colleges to fill its student ranks. Special care was taken, from the president to the faculty, to communicate with junior college faculty and administrators. Frequent face-to-face discussions were arranged between the top administrators of both institutions as well as among the various academic department heads. Personal relationships between UWF and junior college counterparts were extremely important to minimize transfer problems and to ensure appropriate articulation of degree plans. The president of UWF met frequently with the presidents of each of the supporting junior colleges on their own territory. Ultimately, all Florida junior colleges had similar general education requirements, and articulation between junior colleges and UWF was easier. UWF was the first state university to accept junior college graduates without requiring them to repeat courses that they had already taken at their respective junior colleges. These relationships with junior colleges were so important to UWF that the president or an upper-level administrator regularly attended, as an observer and as a resource person, the monthly meetings of the Florida Junior College Presidents Council.

Cluster (Resident) College Concept

Each cluster college was designed to be more than an assemblage of disparate disciplines. In the words of the president, a "living-learning" unit was conceived to encourage personalized faculty-student connections through "counseling, instructional, and living experiences within a given physical complex." The cluster college concept was instituted for many reasons, one of which was to engender a competitive spirit among the three small multidisciplinary colleges. The colleges were encouraged to cultivate competitiveness in an attempt to raise standards. Three colleges of about the same size and encompassing a mix of disciplines made the competitive role more pragmatic. The colleges would compete, for example, to see whose students were better prepared for national tests, which had the most effective student government, which would win the volleyball tournament, and which was most successful in preparing and encouraging students to matriculate into the best graduate schools in their fields. The nature of the colleges' competition is illustrated by the following anecdote. When I was provost of Gamma College, the college faculty and I took great pride in the fact that more UWF accounting majors passed the National Certified Public Accountant Examination on the first attempt than did students from any other state university.

The competitive spirit was lively among the faculty as well. Each college sought to be more effective than the other two in teaching, as well as more active in their respective professional societies and in their contributions to college committees. The faculty from each college expected its provost to acquire a share of the annual budget commensurate with faculty and student accomplishments. Gamma College faculty and students were encouraged to believe that they were the chosen few, the proud, the best and the brightest. College competition and pride was designed to bring out the driving force within each student and to enhance his or her accomplishments.

The choice of disciplines for each college has puzzled many observers. Various discussions on the subject were initiated long before the institution opened, but attempts at agreement led to stalemate. Once individuals were identified as future provosts, the president summoned them to the boardroom and instructed them to stay there until they arrived at an equitable and logical distribution of academic disciplines across the three colleges. Presidential guidelines included the admonition that each college was to have at least one discipline from the sciences, the humanities, the social sciences, education, and business, and that the three colleges should have approximately the same numbers of faculty, students, and budgetary requirements. As the president was about to leave the room, he turned around and, in a Solomonic way, said, "By the way, to ensure you three make no personal deals, I as president shall later determine who will administer which college."

The discipline mix of each college reflects the provosts' efforts to avoid the notions frequently expressed at other universities that "X College is the easiest," "Y College is only interested in the job market," "Z College is too expensive," and so on. Under the cluster college structure at UWF, each college had the responsibility to improve standards in all segments of the college and to ensure that all of the disciplines prepared students for tomorrow's world, not just today's. The aim was to encourage faculty and students trained in different disciplines to learn from one another in order to gain an understanding and appreciation of other disciplines. The faculty might have adjacent offices, work together on college committees, or attend multidisciplinary social events. At most universities, faculty from different disciplines usually never get to meet, let alone talk with, one another. Lifelong friendships grew from this close proximity, and some unpredictable friendships have lasted well beyond retirement.

The cluster college concept was enticing to potential students who envisioned something unique and challenging. They were enthusiastic about joining the "best" college. The sense of belonging and school spirit almost substituted for a Saturday afternoon football game or a fraternity row. The cluster college offered the student an experience unavailable at other universities, and yet they still could major in a field of their choice. The cluster college, upper-level structure, along with the reputation of small classes in which students received individualized attention, a phenomenon that did not exist, in their minds at least, at other state universities, made UWF a sound choice.

Architecture

Each cluster college at UWF had its own architecturally distinctive buildings. The three colleges were isolated by a buffer zone, the University Green. The library, at the center of campus, was designed to be the tallest building on campus. Future buildings were limited in design to one or two stories, to achieve a feeling of intimacy within the large academylike facilities. The two-story dormitories are small and house only two students per suite, thirty-two students per dormitory. They were designed to encourage students to become acquainted with one another. To reinforce the academic mix, students were usually assigned roommates from other disciplines to broaden their academic orientations.

Staff

When staffing the university with its original faculty, we sought candidates who were committed to and even excited about working at this unconventional institution. We did not pursue candidates who were dubious about the university's academic plans. Important details remained to be developed, and the challenges of institution building were intriguing to many of the faculty candidates.

Unlike many other universities, the publish-or-perish policy was not a guideline for faculty advancement. Although faculty were sought for their teaching qualities, those with successful research programs at previous institutions were encouraged to continue their research, but, it was hoped, with undergraduate students at their sides.

In the late 1960s, there was a serious shortage of Ph.D.-trained faculty. Most universities were seeking to fill new faculty positions, and most applicants had more than one offer from which to choose. UWF was not only interested in evaluating an applicant's background and potential for advancement but also concerned about the applicant's commitment to institutional concepts and structure. If it was determined that an applicant under consideration was not completely committed to both the upper-level and the cluster college concepts, the position was usually offered to another who was committed, even when he or she was less experienced. Moreover, since faculty were encouraged to participate in nonacademic college events such as dormitory cookouts and intramural athletic activities, we tried in the interview process to evaluate a candidate's suitability in this area as well. Rarely did an applicant who declined an original offer receive a second chance to join the UWF faculty.

Each college had a guest house where a distinguished professional from outside the university would be encouraged to visit and live among the students for a semester or two. The opportunity to become acquainted with such professionals added a dimension to students' college experience that the faculty and administration believed to be important. The benefit to students varied, depending on individual inclinations and the extent to which they took advantage of the opportunity to interact with the guest, but on the whole we thought the practice worthwhile.

All faculty members within a college were expected to advise students with majors in their respective departments. All students were assigned to a department, and thus a college, according to their declared majors. Advisers were expected to meet regularly with their advisees and were encouraged, in select cases, to invite the students to their homes for social events. Faculty were expected to be role models for their advisees and to assist the students in any reasonable and professional way possible. Involvement with and concern for their advisees, both academic and personal, demonstrated that the university was concerned about its students and did not consider them just computer numbers.

"Esprit de college" persuaded most faculty to become deeply involved in their own college's affairs, particularly with its distinctive array of committees. The action and control, both in and out of the classroom, was at the college level. Colleges frequently took on responsibilities that they felt should be administered at the college level, even if they had to be wrestled away from another division. Faculty gained an appreciation for disciplines far different than their own and certainly disparate from their previous institutions.

Faculty members believed that excellent teaching, research or creative activity (involving students), and college and community service constituted a sure way to tenure and promotion. In time, the residential college concept, later referred to as the cluster college concept, became second nature, taken for granted, and the meticulous recruitment policies were relaxed. Ultimately, younger faculty were employed who were not as dedicated to the cluster college concept as were faculty recruited in the initial years. This slow erosion of faculty commitment to the cluster college concept sowed the seeds for its ultimate demise, as later described here.

Central Administration

Each of the three colleges had to remain within certain administrative confines, some dictated by the state. The need for an overall administrative structure to set parameters and mediate disputes among the colleges was evident. The president recognized that a key to success was to give considerable freedom and authority to each college, although he frequently emphasized that with this responsibility and autonomy came accountability. College-level administrators were responsible for academic programs, housing, and student life, as well as the planning of future college facilities. The position of provost (administrative head of each college) was frequently likened to the presidency of a small college.

Central administration included individuals with titles ranging from coordinators and directors to vice presidents and president. The administration supported the needs of the college faculty and students by making expertise available in the areas of admissions and records, psychological counseling, personnel, public relations, administrative affairs, student affairs, bookstore, library, business office and accounting, purchasing, campus planning, residence hall counseling, student activities, physical plant, development, instructional media, cooperative education and placement, computer services, and continuing education. The heartbeat, control, and action of the university were, from the outset, centered in the colleges rather than the central administration. The academic vice president's role under the cluster college structure was to set broad guidelines and help the colleges improve their programs. The three provosts often banded together and challenged the academic vice president on matters of authority, turf, independence, and management. However, the colleges realized that even under the cluster college design, a central academic vice president was needed to keep the curricula within reasonable limits, to evaluate the provosts, and to give advice to and place limits on the provosts, who periodically tested the bounds of their autonomy. Finally, after three academic vice presidents in about four years, a fourth arrived, one who understood the responsibilities of each college and was confident and secure enough to survive and lead under this structure. Regularly, some members of central administration were reminded that they were there to serve the colleges, their faculties, and students.

The assistant vice president for education (previously called dean of education) provided the university's coordination with local, regional, and state school educators. That office also coordinated student teaching assignments when needed by each college. The position seemed anomalous within the basic cluster college arrangement, and it could have been placed in one of the colleges, but the need for a liaison with outside educators was beyond dispute.

Academic Philosophy

As a main educational theme, the university placed great emphasis on individual student responsibility for educational and extracurricular development. When planning the institution, long before any faculty or administrators had arrived, the president wrote, "The pursuit of truth and the education of enlightened responsible citizens are processes in which human beings must engage as individuals. The opportunity for self-fulfillment, to be a maximum opportunity, must take into account, so far as our understanding and our means will permit, individual strengths, needs, capacities, and desires. Education of the masses to higher and higher levels—a necessary component of the American dream—must not become merely mass production education."

Construction of facilities, including classrooms, focused on the needs of individuals. As a result, classrooms were small, and only one could hold one hundred students. In the absence of meeting rooms to hold classes of three to four hundred students, even if requested by faculty, the university avoided a common complaint voiced by students at other universities: "My classes are too large; I cannot even ask the instructor a question."

Personal attention to students was expected of the faculty. One of the first UWF informational brochures states, "The University of West Florida plans to provide its students with a sound education comparable in its treatment of the individual with the best of the small private colleges in the country, while at the same time making available to the student the resources which only a university can offer." Potential students were told, long before faculty were hired, that their courses would be "presentational—similar to conventional lecture classes, small class seminars, and directed independent study."

Considerable emphasis was placed on education through hands-on experience, and thus UWF, again before any faculty were hired, had a work-study practicum option (cooperative education). And, before the university hired any faculty, administrators were securing work-study positions both locally and nationally in certain academic disciplines where such temporary training positions existed.

Graduate Programs

After the first few months of operation, it became obvious that the institution could not flourish or meet the needs of local industries without graduate programs. An early master's degree program was requested by the U.S. Navy, and, in 1969, after its third year of operation, UWF offered a limited number of master's programs and was accredited by the Southern Association of Colleges and Schools. Soon, master's degree programs were available in most departments, administered by each college. The university avoided a dean of graduate studies. The awarding of graduate degrees at universitywide graduation ceremonies was the responsibility of each college provost and the president. Gradually, this responsibility was centralized, and then the academic vice president and the president awarded the degrees to the master's candidates.

Although most academic departments introduced a master's degree program, some departments chose not to do so, arguing that their efforts were better spent in developing outstanding undergraduate programs. Soon thereafter, their graduates were competing successfully in some of the most prestigious graduate programs in the country.

Housing

Students living on campus (less than half of the student body) were assigned specific college dormitories. Initially, with few exceptions, students assigned to a college's dormitories were members of that college. They were encouraged to seek roommates with dissimilar backgrounds (major, age group, or cultural or ethnic heritage) to broaden personal experiences. Eventually, the number of exceptions to housing-assignment rules increased as students of like ilk (pseudo-fraternity, long-time friends away from home, athletic teams) but of different UWF colleges requested to room together, thus eroding the sovereignty of each college.

Faculty office assignments mixed members of disparate disciplines within the same college. Friendships developed by such proximity have outlasted time and circumstances.

Counteractive Forces to Innovation

Several factors caused the premature demise of the cluster college structure, thus ending the warmth and illumination of this innovative undertaking.

Issues of promotion and tenure, supposedly owing to the disparate discipline mixes, were raised by a few faculty members who felt they were on a slow advancement track. Interdepartmental and intercollege jealousies also kept the cauldron boiling. And some faculty lost their competitive spirit. Frequently, when setbacks occurred, blame was placed on the absence of a conventional "College of . . . " framework.

The strongest challenge to the cluster college structure came from beyond the campus; external professionals and organizations did not always understand the UWF system. Accreditation agencies and professional societies, with few exceptions, had concerns about the structure. Discipline-based accreditation groups, however, apparently had no quarrel with the cluster college concept and were happy to apply their stamp of approval on the departments.

After ten exciting years, the founding president left the university. With the arrival of administrators and faculty not committed to the innovations at UWF, and the establishment of faculty unions throughout all campuses of the state university system of Florida, resulting in a shift in faculty power at UWF, inevitably a conventional structure composed of a college of arts and sciences, a college of education, and a college of business was established in place of the cluster college structure.

Through efforts by faculty with strong research backgrounds, it became impossible for faculty to earn tenure or promotion to the rank of professor based on outstanding teaching, without significant research or creative activity. Further modifications of UWF occurred when a drive to admit freshmen and sophomores doomed the upper-level character of the university. The unique characteristics of UWF were history.

Conclusion

Major innovation, which is foreign to most professionals' experiences, can only exist for a limited time and at a new university. The pressures for conformity eventually tend to outweigh the striving for uniqueness. One needs a rare, imaginative individual, not a committee, to launch an innovative idea.

ALFRED B. CHAET was founding provost of Gamma College at the University of West Florida, Pensacola, and is currently Ford Professor of Physiology at the university.

Metropolitan State University, founded in the inner city to serve largely mature community college transfer students, gives students responsibility for planning their own curricula, with a competence-based focus.

Metropolitan State University

Robert C. Fox, Leah S. Harvey

Metropolitan State University, originally known as Minnesota Metropolitan State College, was authorized as the seventh member of the Minnesota State College System by the Minnesota legislature in June 1971. The idea for an alternative institution of higher education was first proposed in 1969 by G. Theodore Mitau, then chancellor of the state college system. Following the 1971 Citizens' League report "An Urban College: New Kinds of Students on a New Kind of Campus," the legislature appropriated $300,000 to plan and operate a college "center" during the 1972–1973 biennium. David E. Sweet, then vice chancellor for academic affairs for the Minnesota State University System, was appointed by the board as the college's founding president.

The seminal documents that guided the university's initial planning and the development of the college's approach to education were *Prospectus* (Sweet and Moore, 1971) and *Prospectus II* (Minnesota Metropolitan State College, 1971). On the basis of these documents, the college received external funding from the Hill Family Foundation, the United States Office of Education, the Carnegie Corporation, and the Ford and the Bush foundations.

Minnesota Metropolitan State College opened for its first 50 students in February 1972, as a self-conscious experiment in higher education. One year later, the college held its first commencement ceremony for 12 students. The headcount grew from 150 students in 1972, to 1,600 in 1979, to 3,696 in the fall of 1984. Between 1973 and the fall of 1984, 3,639 students graduated from Metro State.

Early changes in the college included a name change in 1975 from Minnesota Metropolitan State College to Metropolitan State University, the 1977 appointment of Reatha Clark King as the second president, and the

NEW DIRECTIONS FOR HIGHER EDUCATION, no. 82, Summer 1993 © Jossey-Bass Publishers

emergence of collective bargaining in 1975 for faculty, administrative and service staff, and classified employees.

In an original planning document, Metro State is described as follows:

> It is a college which admits students and awards them degrees on the basis of demonstrated competence and not on the basis of credit hours accumulated or courses taken. It is a college in which the student has the principal responsibility for designing his or her own educational goals and the means for achieving them, with the personal counsel of readily accessible faculty members whose only responsibility is teaching. It is a college making full use of a great variety of learning resources and teaching techniques and instruments. It is a college which stresses in its curriculum that liberal studies and professional studies can and must be combined in a baccalaureate program so that every student is equipped and has a demonstrated capacity: a) to continue to learn after leaving college, b) to understand and shape his own development as a human being, c) to function as a responsible citizen, d) to utilize lifetime leisure skills, and e) to earn his way in the contemporary, rapidly changing economy [Minnesota Metropolitan State College, 1971, pp. 1–2].

The innovations stemming from this philosophy and the upper-division nature of the university define the uniqueness of this institution.

Upper Division

The upper-division character of Metro State was a political rather than an educational decision. In the years immediately preceding the authorization of Metro State, the state legislature had established six metropolitan area community colleges. Five of these institutions ring the Twin Cities of Minneapolis and Saint Paul, and the other is located near downtown Minneapolis. Thus, the legislature, persuaded that a four-year Metro State would result in unnecessary duplication of first- and second-year efforts and resources in the Twin Cities area, established it as an upper-division degree-completion institution.

This limitation has always been a constraint. Metro State first addressed the issue in 1973 when the university received over $500,000 from the Fund for the Improvement of Postsecondary Education (FIPSE) for a three-year project to extend the Metro State philosophy and process to students in the metropolitan area community colleges. Through the Competence-Based Education (CBE) Project, coordinators were placed in each of the community colleges, and students with less than ninety quarter credits were expected to complete the first portion of their education at the community colleges and then move on to Metro State's B.A. program.

This solution, though, dealt with only a small percentage of Metro State students, since the community colleges represented only about one-fourth of students entering Metro (contrary to many people's expectations), and many of those students were not in the CBE program. Even those students who graduated from the community colleges had diverse backgrounds, since A.A. and A.A.S. degree requirements varied among the community colleges. This variation made the task of developing workable and useful articulation agreements difficult and created pressures on the idea of breadth as a part of B.A. degree programs. Some students entered Metro State as juniors with A.A.S. degrees that were almost exclusively vocational (there was, during the early years of Metro State, a proliferation of two-year vocational programs in the community colleges); others entered ready to start their upper-division concentrations with A.A. degrees representing broad general education; and still others entered with ninety quarter credits earned from a variety of institutions. Metro State, therefore, was forced to offer courses and programs to meet the needs of a wide spectrum of students, ranging from those without any background in literature, history, philosophy, and the like to others ready to begin their accounting and business programs.

Additional tension developed around the upper-division character of Metro State when adult students who did not want to attend community colleges created public pressure on Metro State to respond to their stated needs. With a limited number of Metro State's students coming from the community colleges, the desire to limit duplication and to work coopera- tively often was overshadowed by the desire to have students develop a full four-year curriculum. Although upper division at its inception, Metro State regularly felt pressure to move beyond this narrow range of higher education, and it eventually responded by adding lower-division (for example, the admission of students with less than ninety quarter credits on the basis of their equivalent life and work learning) as well as master's-level programs.

Innovation in General

In addition to the pressures and tensions related to education innovation, Metro State also experienced difficulties as a result of experimenting with other facets of higher education. As the number of students increased, demand for efficiencies became more intense. As more faculty with tradi- tional qualifications and backgrounds were hired, their requests for the usual resources, processes, and perquisites put increased pressure on the innova- tions. The early faculty, having defended the ideals of the institution to conference audiences, visitors, reporters, system office personnel, legisla- tors, the public, funders, and potential and enrolled students, now had to defend their ideas to their colleagues both within the institution and across the Minnesota State University System. Even in an era when individualiza- tion was valued, this defense of innovation was difficult. But as the 1970s gave way to the 1980s and the values of the nation shifted even more in the direction of tradition, the task of defending "differentness" became increasingly frustrating.

Similarly, in the early years of Metro State, there was a sense of being engaged in a working critique of higher education. Faculty and staff came to that task with great enthusiasm, but that enthusiasm proved difficult to sustain for more than a few years.

Specific Innovations and Their Evolution

Because Metro State was established as an alternative to traditional higher education, most practices at the university are innovative. The following examples illustrate some of the more important and substantive of those innovations.

Student Authority. The essence or central element of the Metro State approach to education is defined by the first tenet of the institution: "The college vests in each individual student responsibility for and authority over his/her education. The college vests in its officers and faculty responsibility for and authority over teaching and for determining whether or not a student has given adequate evidence that he/she has achieved his/her educational objectives" (Metropolitan State University, 1980). This tenet placed the student at the center of the educational process in a way virtually unprecedented in higher education. The only institutional requirement was that students complete a planning process in which they analyze their individual backgrounds and competencies and determine what additional competencies, if any, were needed to fulfill B.A. degree requirements. In the first year of Metro State, this planning was conducted either individually or in small groups with advisers (permanent employees who were soon to be called resident faculty members). A student's decisions about his or her own degree program had to be negotiated with and defended before an adviser, faculty and staff reviewers of the program, and, eventually, a final evaluation committee made up of faculty and students.

This arrangement of having students construct their own routes to a B.A. degree changed the typical relationship between faculty and students. Faculty no longer had the coercive power associated with predetermined requirements. Instead, they had only the force of reason and logic, coupled with a willingness and ability to persuade students to make reasonable and rational decisions about the composition of their degree programs. In practical terms, this meant a great deal of individual discussion with students on issues such as the importance of studying literature and philosophy, history, and the arts. For most students, a limited (if any) background in science and mathematics was not a problem—they did not believe that they needed any. "How are these subjects relevant to my work?" was a typical question.

Faculty members, therefore, spent hours trying to persuade students to develop quality B.A. programs. Most students did eventually develop solid and defensible programs. In addition, they had a clear understanding of why they made specific choices and how those choices related to their degrees. The problem was that the energy and commitment required of the faculty could not be maintained with increased numbers of students. The task of repeatedly delivering the same message to an ever-growing body of students became tedious; faculty enthusiasm waned considerably over time.

In February 1974, Metro State replaced the individualized process with the course Individualized Educational Planning (IEP). The development of this course represented a major compromise of the basic tenet of student-centered education. In this course, students did not have complete authority. Rather, students entering Metro State had to enroll in IEP and develop degree plans (representing credits attained before entering Metro State and competencies to be achieved while enrolled at Metro State) that met requirements set by the faculty. Only after compliance with these requirements in the IEP course were students granted authority and responsibility over their degree programs. This deferment of the students' authority represented a compromise between the faculty forces who wanted, and were quite comfortable with, faculty authority and responsibility (as represented by requirements for general education, majors, and degrees) and those who thought that this authority should remain with students. This course is still offered at the university, and the compromise that it reflects remains in effect. The resulting degree programs are not at variance with the conventional programs of higher education.

Overall, the central focus of program development at Metro State remained the individual student, and, even with a ten- to eleven-week IEP course, the planning for each degree program remained essentially individualized, raising the same issues confronted prior to the change in the planning process. As early as 1978, a new faculty member warned that the institution could not afford to maintain its highly individualized approach to degree programs with the more than one thousand students enrolled at that time. Again, the issue of efficiency was coupled with the boredom of redundancy. The process still sapped the energy and commitment of the faculty. It was becoming increasingly difficult for faculty to repeat the same justification for liberal learning, mathematics, and other less popular areas of study that they had repeated a seemingly infinite number of times before. At the very least, it was becoming harder to repeat it with verve, vigor, and passion.

Equally troublesome, as a particular line of reasoning and persuasion was repeated, segments of the faculty came to view the advice not as propositions that were subject to rebuttal but rather as statements of irrefutable truth, givens that could be translated into requirements. For example, if a faculty member in marketing suggested that there are several different ways to become competent in marketing, the advice might be more tentative the first time that it was offered than it would be after several years of thinking about what a person needs to achieve competence, and after having repeated the various ideas and suggestions innumerable times. Some faculty at Metro became more comfortable mandating curricula.

Another concern, raised by faculty new to the institution, was the perception that the persuasion process (as opposed to requirements) was essentially dishonest. Since faculty were trying to persuade, they must have some end (or perhaps some image of a B.A. degree) in mind. By not telling students about that end and letting them in on "the secret" only one little piece at a time, faculty were acting deceptively and dishonestly. Thus, according to this argument, faculty should just remove this facade, set out requirements immediately, and let students get to work on learning. Although the new faculty did not prevail completely with this argument, their continued pressure moved the university toward a more conventional framework of degree requirements.

Finally, students also brought pressure against their own complete authority and responsibility. When Metro State first opened, a large number of students welcomed the opportunity to enroll in an innovative institution. The university was inundated with self-directed learners who had prior college experience and were ready to plan and complete their own degree programs. Whether because of the times or a new kind of clientele, students in the 1980s were more comfortable with, and accepting of, faculty and institutional authority than were Metro State's first students in the 1960s and early 1970s.

Individualized Learning Contracts. One dimension of Metro State's innovation had to do with learning contracts and individualized learning projects. While described in the early materials, and fairly typical of most learning during the first two years of Metro State's operation, this aspect of innovation has not predominated Metro State's education philosophy and practice.

Metro State was (and remains) competence-based, and learning contracts were developed in response to this focus. Courses were developed within two years of Metro State's beginning, but the emphasis was on individualized learning within the classroom. The terminology used, *group learning opportunities* instead of *classes*, and *competencies* rather than *credits*, was often perceived to reflect a disdain of classes. In fact, from the beginning, Metro State staff encouraged students to take classes at other institutions to achieve the particular competencies that Metro was not able to address. In the end, though, student interest in group learning, faculty disinterest in repetition, and the need for efficiency led to increased reliance on courses. In 1975, 20 to 25 percent of all student registrations were in courses. That figure increased to 54 percent by 1979 and to 75 percent in 1985.

Prior Learning Evaluation. As a competence-based institution, emphasizing learning outcomes rather than process, Metro State has always recognized prior, nonclassroom learning. At the outset, the university accepted students who had completed ninety quarter credits or who had the equivalent of ninety quarter credits in prior, nonclassroom learning. With that program, more than 60 percent of credits recorded on transcripts were for prior learning. When the program was phased out and only upper-division learning could be recorded, the numbers of credits for prior learning decreased rapidly. Few students gained the theoretical knowledge expected at the upper-division level from nonclassroom experience. By 1979, the number of credits awarded for prior, nonclassroom learning had decreased to 11 percent of the overall credits awarded. This change was of concern, since students with significant practical knowledge were taking courses solely to gain the theory needed to complement that knowledge. Thus, some students were spending unnecessary time in the classroom. The situation was also difficult for instructors, who had to accommodate a range of students, from those with no knowledge in a field to those with extensive practical knowledge. To address this problem, in 1983 two faculty members submitted a grant proposal to FIPSE to develop theory seminars—short courses designed to augment prior practical learning with theory.

Community Faculty. The nature of the faculty is one of the most important aspects of Metro State as a community-based institution. Metro's planners projected that most of the teaching and the evaluation of student performance (including informing students about real-world expectations in certain work areas) would be done by community faculty, and that most of the advising and the curriculum development and program planning would be done by full-time advisers (later called resident faculty). The intention was not to develop a cadre of adjunct faculty but rather to fully utilize community resources in the educational process. The university believed (correctly, for most subject areas) that there was a sufficient number of appropriately degreed persons working in the community who would be willing and able to teach occasionally for Metro State. As a competence-based institution, however, the university sometimes selected highly competent people to teach, consult with, and evaluate students in some areas, even though these instructors lacked traditional academic degrees. The resident faculty developed criteria for judging the expert status of individuals for purposes of serving as community faculty members. These criteria allowed people with and without traditional academic degrees to qualify, although the hiring of individuals without degrees has always been the exception rather than the rule.

The use of community faculty was based on the belief that students must understand both the theoretical and the practical elements of a particular subject. Instructors with actual practice in the field of the subject area taught would thus bring something special to the teaching-learning relationship. Additionally, many early Metro State staff were hesitant to embrace traditional higher education and believed that serious, trained, competent practitioners, unlike traditional faculty, would understand the ways in which theories did and did not work in practice and would be able to inform students about the latest changes and developments in their particular fields.

The university sponsored regular orientation, training, and professional development activities for community faculty. The aim was to help instructors acquire the skills needed to be excellent teachers and to give them the opportunity to be part of an academic collegial environment. As it turned out, the community faculty were also less expensive than the eventually unionized resident faculty, and they allowed for faster administrative and faculty adaptation and change (curriculum and otherwise).

The notion that academically prepared practitioners could and should provide the main teaching function for the institution was not without its problems, however. Many of these persons were not competent teachers (although this is often true of professional full-time educators as well). Many were teaching for the first time and had not approached their own education with the intention of developing their abilities as teachers. They had not considered all of the elements of a well-designed syllabus as a teaching tool or the many approaches to fostering quality learning. Finally, many of these individuals with prior teaching experience had never taught adult students.

In addition, different content areas presented different instructional needs. For example, the primary disciplines of the humanities and the arts and sciences have limited direct vocational and professional applicability in areas other than academe. Many people in these disciplines pursue graduate work in order to teach, not to work outside of academe. Application in their subject areas is usually academic research, not work in the nonacademic marketplace. Thus, for example, the task of finding historians to teach history on a part-time basis for Metro State while doing other things on a full-time basis was more difficult than finding advertising or public relations professionals to teach in their areas of expertise. And, indeed, if such a historian were found, he or she would likely want to be a full-time faculty member. Thus, use of community faculty varied across disciplines.

Community-Based Classrooms. As a community-based institution, Metro State relied on the use of community facilities. Original planning documents described this feature of community-based education in terms of fuller use of public buildings and resources, such as nighttime use of public schools and other government buildings (Minnesota Metropolitan State College, 1971, p. 15). Thus, the early Metro State was everywhere—classes were offered at over one hundred sites throughout the Twin Cities. While some of these sites were free or low cost, others were rented at market rates. The tracking of quarter-to-quarter variations in space availability as well as the scheduling and confirmation of facilities became an expensive staff function.

Apart from the costs and difficulties of finding and confirming classroom space, notifying students, and so on, a host of other issues put pressure on the use of community-based classrooms. Teaching and learning support (often rooms lacked writing boards, audiovisual adaptability, and proper lighting), adult student comfort (chairs, desks, and tables for adults rather than grade school children), access (Metro's holiday schedules did not always match those of its various lessors and donors, and janitors sometimes forgot that there would be a Metro State class on one night or another), and legal matters (insurance coverage and responsibility for protecting, closing, and locking the sites) all contributed to change in Metro State's practices. So also did the issue of visibility and public image. Specifically, since the university could not put signage on short-term leased or donated facilities, there was no physical image of Metro State in the public's mind, including potential students and donors.

The energy crisis was perhaps the crowning blow to Metro's community-based classrooms. In the search for an alternative approach, President Reatha Clark King presided over the development of a corridor plan whereby nearly all classes would be held in facilities either in downtown Minneapolis, downtown Saint Paul, or the corridor between the two downtown areas, with long-term leases and fewer facilities. Very shortly after the implementation of this plan, Metro State was offered a physical plant. A vacated hospital site, controlled by the Saint Paul Port Authority (the public financing arm of the city of Saint Paul), was donated for one dollar to the Minnesota State University System as the headquarters and principal administrative site for Metro State.

Given Metro's growing enrollment, the opportunity to consolidate classroom space was welcomed by most staff. Fewer sites with more classrooms per site offered improved access to audiovisual materials, an array of learning spaces better suited to teaching and learning needs, increased communication among and between students and instructors in different classes, and a sense of community not previously possible. Predictability and continuity were evident.

Another community-based dimension of Metro State that has prospered is the library and information systems function of the university. Community library systems have been used as the Metro State library resources from the beginning, not only because of their quality, availability to all citizens, and branch distribution throughout the metropolitan area, much like Metro State's classroom facilities, but also because they are a key to lifelong learning. According to Metro's philosophy, if people learned or were reinforced in using the public library systems as students, perhaps they would continue to use the resources of the various libraries as they pursued learning throughout the rest of their lives. An interlibrary loan system, available in virtually all libraries in the Twin Cities, and computer-accessible catalogues made this approach possible. A primary function of the Metro "library" was to help students develop the skills and inclination to use these resources. Thus, workshops, materials and handouts, faculty training on integrating library projects into class syllabi, and continued instruction about ways in which to use the libraries became Metro State's primary library activities. Library staff also helped faculty obtain requisite journals and similar continuing education and scholarly materials in their disciplines.

One problem with Metro State's approach to library and information systems is that the wide, multisite array of library systems and resources is difficult for many people to understand and grasp. Thus, people have said that Metro State does not have a library, a particularly damning statement for a university. This criticism, along with complaints from state officials and others who prefer traditional campus libraries, has caused problems. Similarly, access to the interlibrary loan system assumed a collection that was shared, and various policies and administrative activities have been necessary to ensure Metro State's continued access to this system. In spite of these pressures, however, the use of community-based library systems as the university's library has endured.

Conclusion

The early years of Metro State were characterized by the vigor and intensity of commitment to principles (even though the principles were often controversial and not understood in the same way by everyone). Principles were maintained even when contrary to the demands of students, faculty, and external publics. There was a vision of the core values of teaching and learning and of how higher education should be conducted.

As Metro State grew, the institution developed its own persona, and student and public demands were heard differently. Efficiency became a recognized value. Metro State became an accepted member of the Minnesota and national education community, with all of the pressures and tensions associated with being accepted and acceptable. Nonetheless, the central founding ideas and ideals are still at work.

References

Metropolitan State University. *North Central Association Self-Study Report.* Saint Paul, Minn.: Metropolitan State University, 1980.

Minnesota Metropolitan State College. *Prospectus II.* Saint Paul: Minnesota Metropolitan State College, 1971.

Minnesota Metropolitan State College. *Self-Study Report.* Saint Paul: Minnesota Metropolitan State College, 1975.

Sweet, D. E., and Moore, D. R. *Minnesota Metropolitan State College Prospectus.* Saint Paul: Minnesota Metropolitan State College, 1971.

ROBERT C. FOX, *one of the founding faculty, coordinates the education planning process at Metropolitan State University, Saint Paul, Minnesota.*

LEAH S. HARVEY, *academic affairs vice president, started as a faculty member at Metropolitan State in 1975.*

With a commuter student body averaging thirty years of age and a faculty trained at leading graduate schools, a new upper-level institution created a culture of commitment to teaching and student learning.

University of Texas of the Permian Basin

V. Ray Cardozier

The Texas legislature authorized the establishment of the University of Texas of the Permian Basin (UTPB) in 1969 as an upper-level institution, to admit only juniors, seniors, and graduate students. The president and vice presidents for academic affairs and business affairs arrived in Odessa in the summer of 1970, and the institution opened in 1973, allowing three full years for planning.

As it turned out, three years were needed, due in part to litigation contesting title to the property where the campus was to be built, brought by five residents of Midland, 20 miles east of Odessa. The city of Midland had hoped to have the university located midway between the two cities, in Midland County (for details on the struggle over the location of the university, see Cardozier, 1988). The long planning period gave the officers ample opportunity to undertake studies and to develop policies and plans that would institute several innovations, in addition to the upper-level model.

Odessa is located 350 miles west of Dallas, toward El Paso, on the arid plains of West Texas, and is the center of the oil industry from which the institution's name was drawn. The area was settled by ranchers in the 1880s, although with rainfall averaging thirteen inches per year, ranching is poor, requiring as much as forty acres per animal. But, in 1923, oil was discovered and the Permian Basin became the largest oil-producing area in the country, rapidly swelling the population with people to serve the oil industry. Odessa was settled largely by blue-collar workers—roughnecks, roustabouts, tool pushers, and other laborers in the oil industry—and Midland by white-collar workers, particularly geologists, engineers, lawyers, and other college-educated persons.

NEW DIRECTIONS FOR HIGHER EDUCATION, no. 82, Summer 1993 © Jossey-Bass Publishers

In 1970, the population of Odessa was approximately 80,000, and Midland was 60,000; county populations were about 93,000 and 65,000, respectively. Both towns grew rapidly in the latter part of the decade as the oil industry boomed following the rapid rise in the price of oil from the Middle East oil cartel. By the mid-1980s, the oil boom had faded and growth came to a halt; with high unemployment, both counties experienced an exodus of workers. In the 1990 census, however, the industry had stabilized and Ector County (Odessa) had a population of 118,954, and Midland County had 106,611. Together with surrounding counties within commuting distance of Odessa, the population totaled more than 300,000. Prior to the opening of UTPB, the closest baccalaureate institutions were Angelo State University, 130 miles to the east, and Texas Tech University, 140 miles to the north.

Although the student revolution on college campuses in the 1960s had been highly destructive, it had also made the academic world acutely aware of deficiencies in colleges and universities. UTPB planners envisioned an institution that would try to correct as many of these deficiencies as possible. The University of Texas System Board of Regents and administration were intensely involved in establishing several other campuses at the same time and allowed the administration of UTPB considerable freedom in developing plans for the institution.

This chapter examines some of the plans for UTPB during its first ten years of operation and assesses the outcomes of the various innovations and other policies and practices that departed from the higher education norm. Most were not innovations in a strict sense, that is, totally new, but rather were departures from the norm; in some cases, the practices have long been found in small private liberal arts colleges but are rare in state colleges and universities.

Organization and Administration

UTPB was created as an upper-level institution for students transferring from community colleges. One community college already existed in Odessa, another in Big Spring, fifty-five miles away—a short commute for most West Texans—and one was scheduled to open in Midland in 1970. Unfortunately, calculation of the number of students who transfer from community colleges in the area to degree-granting institutions was badly flawed; reportedly, the planning staff of the state coordinating board calculated accurately, but the politically led board essentially tripled the estimate before the planning document went to press to make the upper-level school more palatable to the legislature. In 1976, the state coordinating board data showed that transfers from the three community colleges—which then had a combined enrollment of more than seventy-two hundred—to degree-granting institutions in a typical fall semester totaled about six hundred, half of whom had completed less than sixty credits and were, therefore, ineligible to enroll in an upper-level institution.

But lack of students is not the main problem with the upper-level model; its major deficiencies are academic. By the early 1980s, all four of the upper-level universities in Florida, on which the upper-level institutions in Texas had been modeled, had added freshman and sophomore years, not because they lacked students but because they wanted to better serve students academically (for more on the upper-level model, see Cardozier, 1984). In 1991, the legislature added freshman and sophomore years at UTPB, having done so earlier for the University of Texas at Dallas and Corpus Christi State University, which had also opened as upper-level institutions.

Chairs. One of the major criticisms of large, and some small, institutions is that they lack coherence; walls develop between departments, and faculty know little about the work of other disciplines. In an attempt to minimize this problem, original plans for UTPB called for no departments or chairs; instead each discipline would be led by a program coordinator. All financial administration would be centered in the office of the dean of the college (there were three colleges), and the program coordinator would be responsible only for program development and leadership, as is common in some small liberal arts colleges. It soon became apparent that the program coordinator should be named chairman of the faculty of the discipline in order to recruit more capable faculty to serve in that role, individuals who would not accept appointments with the title of program coordinator. However, the term *faculty* (as in Faculty of History) was used instead of *department*.

Graduate Study. From the standpoint of the planners, the traditional organization in most U.S. universities, in which a separate administrative organization is created for graduate study, is a mistake. Typically, a graduate dean is responsible for graduate education but has no budget for it; on the other hand, the dean of the college or academic division is responsible for the faculty and the budget that support graduate education but is not in a direct line of responsibility for graduate study. Department faculties communicate directly with the graduate dean concerning admission of students, degree requirements, and most other matters regarding graduate education.

At UTPB, deans of colleges were responsible for both graduate and undergraduate education, and the vice president for academic affairs assumed responsibilities performed by the graduate dean in more traditional graduate education organizations. This arrangement was facilitated by three factors: there was no lower division, virtually all of the faculty held terminal degrees, and no teaching assistants were employed to teach classes. With deans of colleges controlling budgets and other matters influencing graduate education, they were as attentive to graduate studies as to undergraduate studies, and the arrangement worked exceedingly well. Although a few other institutions had long had similar organizations for graduate education, the idea is now being considered more widely, as it provides a more rational system for the administration of graduate education.

Teacher Education. The planners saw teacher education as the responsibility of the entire faculty rather than the teacher education faculty alone. Toward that end, a college of arts and education was established in which members of the faculty of teacher education were on a par with faculties of liberal arts, all of whom helped determine teacher education policies and worked closely with the teacher education faculty.

Although about one-third, and later one-fourth, of the students were preparing for teaching, no degree in education was established. Instead, students preparing for teaching took their degrees in liberal arts or science and took their education courses—four courses and student teaching for secondary certification—as electives. For those preparing for teaching in elementary schools, a minor in teacher education was developed. The teacher education faculty found the arrangement quite satisfactory, and although some school administrators in West Texas did not adjust quickly to the lack of bachelor's degrees in education, graduates did not experience discrimination in the job market. Also, as planned, the faculties in liberal arts and the sciences became heavily involved in teacher education. This organization for teacher education is common in many liberal arts colleges; however, in view of the fact that West Texas is very traditional, the practices departed from the norm among state institutions and thus, for the context and the time, constituted a bold step.

Year-Round Enrollment. As explained later, several alternative approaches to teaching made it possible for students to enroll and begin their studies at any time during the year. When the institution opened in 1973, Vietnam War veterans were leaving the military services and often wished to enroll at midsemester. The policy of year-round admissions attracted considerable attention, and a few students did enroll at midsemester, but most students enrolled during regular registration periods. This policy produced difficulty with the state coordinating board in that enrollments at times other than designated registration periods were applied, for funding purposes, to the accounting of the subsequent semester. Occasionally, a student would enroll in the middle of a semester for several self-paced courses and then enroll at the beginning of the next semester for a full course load, both of which were reported together to the coordinating board, which required explanation.

Teaching

Perhaps no issue advanced by the student revolution of the late 1960s and early 1970s attracted more attention than the lack of attention to undergraduate teaching. The planners of UTPB set out to make teaching paramount and to create a climate that would encourage faculty to join in this effort. As explained later, several steps were taken to achieve this, and by all accounts the institution was successful.

Self-Paced Instruction. The planners knew that a large percentage of the student body would be part-time, but this was not the sole reason for turning to alternative approaches to teaching. Heavy emphasis was placed initially on self-paced instruction, and the Keller Plan. In brief, the plan consists of organizing a course by units, which a student studies independently, meeting periodically with a professor for tutorials; the student must pass a test on each unit before proceeding to the next unit. Each faculty member was asked to teach at least one course on a self-paced basis in the opening year, and all did so.

In the first year, more than 30 percent of the course registrations were in self-paced courses; however, within five years, the number had declined to about 10 percent. Academically, self-paced instruction was a success. It had the added advantage of permitting students whose jobs required travel, for example, airline pilots, to complete courses and make progress toward a degree. But it suffered from two problems: First, it was extremely demanding on faculty, requiring many hours more per student than were required in organized classes; as a result, only those faculty who were dedicated to self-paced instruction pursued it assiduously after the first year. Second, students allocated their time to organized classes, first, and delayed completion of self-paced courses. A few students completed their self-paced coursework in a few weeks, as the planners had envisioned, but the majority required more than one semester, often two or more, to complete self-paced courses. In evaluations, students approved of self-paced courses with respect to the learning achieved, but they said that the lack of externally imposed discipline was a deficiency.

Contract Study. Again with the intent of serving part-time students, contract study was instituted, following the pattern of Evergreen State College and several other institutions. Contract study is independent study but with a difference; prior to undertaking the study, the student writes a detailed plan of what he or she plans to study, the learning to be achieved, and how the study will be carried out. This plan must be approved by the supervising professor in writing before the student begins study. It avoids the ambiguity and lack of direction of most independent study. Academically, the process worked well at UTPB, but it had the same two deficiencies as self-paced instruction.

The laboratories were organized on a self-paced basis so that students could complete their laboratory exercises at any time, even weekends and nights. This was useful to students who were employed and also for students who sought to improve their learning by repeating experiments. However, the practice proved too expensive to staff, and when funds became scarce, it was necessary to eliminate assistants who supervised the laboratories on weekends and evenings, although some flexibility was maintained for students who could not attend scheduled laboratory periods.

Laboratories for earth sciences, chemistry, life sciences, physics, and engineering were housed together without walls. The intent of the planners was to allow students, while they were conducting laboratory exercises, to observe experiments under way in other fields as a means of stimulating curiosity about those disciplines and enhancing their understanding of science. The results were only moderately successful; moreover, the openness of the laboratories led to such a high incidence of theft that it became necessary to provide security systems that thwarted the original intent of mutual observation and learning.

Modular Classrooms. All internal walls of classrooms consisted of modular panels that could be installed and removed easily, making it possible to reconfigure classrooms and teaching space in a matter of hours. All classrooms were initially open on at least one side, and corner classrooms were open on two sides, in an attempt to make teaching an open process and to stimulate interest of passersby. The plan was most popular with teacher education faculty, since it was similar to the open-classroom concept widely applied in elementary and secondary schools around the country. But noise in hallways forced the closing of some of the classrooms; further, the openness was not as useful as anticipated. The modular walls proved popular with new deans and other administrators who wanted to reconfigure their offices.

As already noted, the term *department* was shunned in an attempt to foster interdisciplinary interest and minimize disciplinary balkanization. Other terminology was adopted that more accurately described the various faculties and disciplines; for example, the Faculty (instead of Department) of English, College of Management (instead of Business Administration), pedagogical studies (instead of education), and earth sciences, which included geology and other related studies (instead of geology).

Several other ideas for improving the curriculum or instructional process, most of them not unique or even rare but certainly unconventional, never got beyond the planning stage. Some of these ideas were formulated when, in 1971, it appeared that the legislature would add freshman and sophomore years prior to the opening of the institution. For example, plans were made to require every graduating senior to demonstrate proficiency in one lifetime sport, that is, a game played alone or with not more than one other person, such as swimming, golf, tennis, and handball. The intent was to develop proficiency and interest in a physical activity that could be pursued for a lifetime, in contrast to team sports, which are usually abandoned when people leave college. But, without freshmen and sophomores, and in view of the fact that all undergraduates had already met physical education course requirements elsewhere, this plan was dropped.

Also when four-year status appeared likely, plans were made for the teaching of composition and rhetoric by the Faculty of Communication, rather than the Faculty of English. Some sections of freshman composition were to be taught by journalists and other professional writers, each focusing on a subject theme such as sports, science, technology, politics, or the environment in order to capitalize on students' interests as a way to teach basic writing skills. Sections focusing on traditional literary writing were also considered.

Initial plans also called for senior seminars (one for the humanities, another for the social sciences, and so on) in which students would look at their fields of study in relation to society and its problems, an idea similar to that recommended fifteen years later by Boyer (1987) in *College: The Undergraduate Experience in America*. There was also consideration of an exit examination in writing and another in conversational speaking as qualifications for a baccalaureate degree. While faculty members found the aims laudable, they were reluctant to undertake the examinations.

In most universities, graduate class meetings of three hours once a week are common, but the planners felt that at the master's level, class meetings of one and one-half hours twice a week would be more effective. After following that policy for several years, most faculty agreed that the schedule was more effective than once-a-week classes; however, students, many of whom commuted great distances, opposed the policy, and, eventually, graduate classes were changed to the traditional schedule of one three-hour meeting per week. In short, the policy was sound pedagogically but vulnerable to change for practical reasons, as was the case for so many of the innovative ideas at UTPB.

The planners also considered developing an attribute profile of each student, in addition to letter grades, based on the proposition that such information might be as beneficial, if not more so, to prospective employers as a record of academic achievement. In addition to grades for academic achievement, instructors would also evaluate all of their students on factors such as verbal ability, writing ability, initiative, organization, human relations skills, creativity, and judgment. Faculty found these proposed evaluations to be beyond their competence and thus opposed the plan.

Another idea, considered only briefly when four-year status appeared likely in 1971, had to do with football. The planners recognized the conflict between the ideal and reality in American college football. They were also aware of the fact that West Texans take their football seriously and would not tolerate a team that did not win (for insight into high school football in West Texas and the fervor of its fans, see Bissinger, 1990). This led to discussion of a plan that included payments to football players, if not salaries equivalent to their worth, then at least at an hourly rate equivalent to the payscale of students who worked part-time at the university. The administration of football would have been placed under an office of public relations, in keeping with the primary function of big-time football in universities today. Finally, players would not have been required to take a full academic load during football season. Instead, they would have taken only the number of credits that they could reasonably be expected to complete satisfactorily. But all of this never got beyond the brainstorming stage for several reasons, including the fact that neither of the two national athletic associations would have approved and a schedule of games would have been difficult to arrange. Yet, the idea continued to be discussed among faculty and administrators for some time, especially since it promised to deal with football more honestly than is the case in many universities.

Faculty

No aspect of the planning process demanded more of the time, energy, and thought of the initial staff than the recruitment and selection of faculty. The staff recognized that whatever the institution achieved would depend largely on the quality of the faculty. Fortunately, the selection of faculty got under way at a time when a surplus of Ph.D. graduates was beginning to develop. As a consequence, the university was able to attract many faculty of outstanding talent.

During the first year of planning, the president and the vice president for academic affairs visited dozens of campuses of leading universities all over the country, seeking ideas and interviewing prospective deans and senior faculty. By the beginning of the second planning year, the deans had arrived, and, together with the officers already present, they stepped up the planning for faculty recruitment. There was unanimous agreement among all of the planners, with the concurrence of the University of Texas System administration, that an attempt would be made to recruit faculty who had been trained in the leading research universities in the country. The reasons were several. In the beginning, the staff did not have specialists in all disciplines and were therefore unable to assess personally the disciplinary competence of prospective faculty. This is not to suggest that scholarly or scientific competence was ignored in recruiting; quite the contrary. Considerable inquiry was made about each candidate's disciplinary competence, but the reputation of the department in which the candidate had been trained was a major factor. The assumption was made that, on balance, individuals who received their Ph.D. degrees from leading graduate schools were more likely to be competent in their disciplines, and that the chances of appointing individuals who were not competent in their disciplines would be reduced by this policy. Except for business administration, in which there was at the time a severe shortage of Ph.D. faculty, most of the faculty appointed had received a Ph.D. at one of the top twenty-five or thirty graduate schools in the country.

In spite of the remote location and the less than sterling image of the "oil patch," at least by Texas standards, a stellar collection of faculty was assembled by opening day, attracted by the institution's innovative plans, especially its emphasis on teaching. They held Ph.D. degrees from Wisconsin, Iowa, Ohio State, Harvard, Yale, Chicago, California Institute of Technology, Northwestern, the University of California at Los Angeles and at

Berkeley, and other comparable institutions.

It was also assumed that individuals who held degrees from leading graduate schools were likely to be more sophisticated intellectually and to have higher expectations for their students. The expectations were that these faculty members would bring broad intellectual horizons to their teaching and that when students sought guidance for graduate study, these faculty would be more likely to recommend leading graduate schools for their more capable students. Both expectations were fulfilled.

The planners focused heavily on teaching competence as a requirement for faculty appointment. By selecting faculty who had been trained in leading graduate schools, who were competent in their disciplines, recruiters could devote more time and attention to assessing a candidate's potential with respect to teaching, interest in students, and the broader role of faculty. The recruiters visited dozens of campuses and interviewed hundreds of potential candidates; they also conducted interviews at professional conferences. For example, more than fifty individuals were interviewed for the first three positions in history. After a short-list had been developed, five or more references of each candidate were interviewed, usually by telephone, at least two of whom were persons not listed by the candidate. Letters of recommendation were rarely requested because of their poor validity. Finally, three to five candidates were brought to Odessa for two- to three-day interviews.

In all interviews and conversations with references, emphasis was placed on the candidate's performance, or promise in the case of Ph.D. candidates, as teachers, their empathy for students, and their perception of the faculty role. In their visits to Odessa, candidates not only were interviewed by university administrators and other faculty but also were entertained by local citizens. (One of the advantages of building a new university in a town for the first time is the excitement and enthusiasm of local citizens about the enterprise; Odessans were generous with their time and money in helping to build the university, including recruitment of faculty and staff.)

The hard work and attention to detail in the recruitment of faculty yielded success beyond the planners' dreams. The faculty enthusiastically adopted the teaching ethos and worked hard to make it a reality. Several practices helped to underscore the institution's commitment to teaching, including salary adjustments. The highlight of the annual honors convocation was the award to the outstanding teacher of the year. In formal and informal assessments of teaching, students were exceptionally laudatory about the quality of teaching and the faculty attentiveness to students and their needs. Students voiced high praise for faculty competence in their disciplines and as teachers.

Some years later, I discussed the faculty selection policy with the chancellor of a similar institution established in Texas at the same time, whose policy was to recruit faculty who had been trained in second-level graduate schools. He argued that the students served by both of our institutions— mostly older, part-time, place-bound, and, usually, low socioeconomic level—were culturally more comfortable with such faculty. However, I am still persuaded that the UTPB policy was sound. The policy was discussed many times with groups of students, who strongly supported it because of the superior competence of their teachers; whatever cultural differences existed were irrelevant to the students. The disadvantage was high faculty turnover. The caliber of faculty recruited inevitably led to the loss of some after three or four years to much better institutions. The planners had foreseen this hazard, however, and believed that in spite of the problem of continually having to recruit new faculty, students benefited by their exposure to highly capable faculty.

Research. Another reason for selecting faculty who had been trained at leading graduate schools had to do with research. The planners, all of whom had received Ph.D. degrees from leading research universities and whose prior posts had been in such institutions, were committed to research as a function of every university. However, they agreed that not all faculty, even in research universities, are productive researchers, and that efforts to require all faculty to be productive in research, especially in regional state universities, had not been successful. In recruiting faculty who had been trained at leading graduate schools, the assumption was that these individuals, having been socialized in academic environments where all faculty were expected to be involved in research, would see research as an inherent component of the academic ethos and thus would engage in research not as a requirement but as an expression of their perception of the role of a university faculty member.

With this prior socialization in mind, the planners developed a policy in which evaluation based on research productivity was optional. The decision was entirely the choice of the faculty member. If he or she chose to be evaluated on research and publication, a reduced teaching load was allowed, and at evaluation time the faculty member was evaluated on his or her research productivity as well as teaching and service. If the individual chose not to be evaluated on research, he or she carried a full teaching load and was evaluated solely in terms of teaching and service.

Some years later, the administration evaluated the policy and concluded that it had worked out essentially as planned. To the surprise of the planners, only about half of the faculty chose the research option; others explained that they were engaged in research and published but were willing to carry a heavier teaching load for the privilege of not being under pressure to produce research quickly. The research productivity of those who carried a full teaching load was only slightly less than that of those who chose the research option.

During an accreditation visit by a team from the Southern Association of Colleges and Schools, the evaluators concluded that the UTPB faculty productivity in papers read at professional conferences and published journal articles, books and chapters of books, and monographs was about the same as in comparable institutions that had a publish-or-perish policy for all faculty. The lowest research productivity was found among the faculties of business and education, both of whom were engaged significantly in consulting with business or working with the public schools. In the fine arts, artistic creativity was equated with research.

Tenure. After much deliberation, the planners chose to experiment with a term appointment plan, which became known locally as term tenure. Assistant professors were appointed and evaluated annually, during which time they might be terminated, with a year's notice. During their sixth year, a decision was made as to whether they would be retained. If the decision was to continue, they were given a seven-year term contract with the same conditions as conventional tenure. The decision was made not later than the second year in the case of associate and full professors. During the sixth year of a seven-year term appointment, evaluation was conducted by a faculty committee. If the faculty member's service was judged satisfactory, he or she was given another seven-year contract; if not, their appointment expired. (They were not dismissed; rather, their contract was not renewed, a technical but important difference.)

It was believed that a term contract would motivate faculty to avoid declines in their performance. As a seven-year contract neared its end, the faculty member would conduct a self-assessment, often with the counsel of chairs, deans, and senior faculty, and attempt to correct deficiencies, if any. This, indeed, proved to be the case; several faculty whose performances had lagged began in their fifth year to improve; by the time the committee reviewed them in the sixth year, they were performing satisfactorily. The policy has been criticized by some writers because it failed to deny reappointment to anyone. On the contrary; it was not the intent of the planners that anyone fail to be reappointed. Rather, the policy was designed as a mechanism for motivating faculty to assess their performance periodically and to make necessary improvements, and it accomplished that goal.

All faculty candidates were informed of the policy before they were appointed. Some who had interviewed at institutions with tenure quotas were fascinated by the policy, but after a few years at UTPB, the majority indicated that they preferred conventional tenure. As one observer expressed, "Why would anyone given the choice of lifetime job security versus a seven-year contract not choose the former?" The policy was later changed by a subsequent administration that was more comfortable with traditional tenure.

Faculty Evaluation. Faculty evaluation was conducted in a fairly conventional manner, by committees usually composed of five colleagues of equal or higher rank than the individual evaluated. Considerable emphasis was placed on documentary material: syllabi, teaching notes, examinations, and the like. Based on an innovative policy developed during the planning stage, deans, chairs, and full professors were at liberty to visit any class without prior notice. If the purpose was to evaluate teaching, two such visits were required as a way of avoiding an assessment based on observation of a single, atypical teaching performance. The practice was not exercised often; it varied with the personal inclinations of deans, chairs, and full professors whenever they were serving on evaluation committees. Overall, the policy worked as planned and was effective in the evaluations of faculty, but it was not used as widely as some planners had envisioned.

Cognate Teaching. One of the continuing problems in academe is disciplinary insularity, specialization at the expense of a broad, general education. The planners, in seeking mechanisms to broaden student interest beyond their own disciplines, hoped that this end might be achieved, in part, if each faculty member annually taught one course unrelated to his or her own discipline. It was postulated that if students in business administration, for example, saw their faculty members teaching courses in music, sociology, and other disciplines, they would be stimulated to broaden their education. Several faculty members did teach in other disciplines, based on expertise gained in graduate school through a minor field of study, undergraduate study, or some other avenue. But the policy was not broadly adopted. It is the nature of graduate education that an individual focuses on a single discipline and, indeed, a specialty within that discipline. As a result, most faculty did not feel competent to teach in another discipline, nor were they interested in doing so. The administration did not press the policy, lest some faculty attempt to teach courses for which they were unqualified.

Interdisciplinary Faculty Offices. Even though UTPB was a small institution—enrollment did not exceed two thousand in the first ten years—the faculty tended to associate primarily with others in their own respective disciplines. Efforts were made to find ways to stimulate interaction among faculty of different disciplines, both for the benefit of faculty and to encourage students to broaden their education. A policy was established that faculty of different disciplines share offices. Full professors were provided private offices, but assistant and associate professors and others shared offices, two per large office. The two were from different colleges as well. Thus, an engineer shared an office with a philosopher, a musician with a life scientist, a kinesiologist with a teacher of business law, and so on.

Most faculty found the experience stimulating; from their office mates and their office mates' students they learned a great deal about other disciplines outside their own colleges. The only objection came from the management faculty, who eventually voted to share offices among themselves.

Library

The director of the library arrived in the summer of 1971, two years before the institution opened. In addition to training and experience as a university librarian, he had served as director of a computer center—a fortuitous combination, for he proceeded to computerize the library from the beginning, including using computer data bases from vendors and dealers; automated ordering, receiving and fund accounting, cataloguing and processing through the Ohio Computing Library Center system, a public catalogue; and embedded security control in books, all commonplace in libraries now but still new at that time. Indeed, UTPB was reportedly the first institution in Texas to have a fully automated library.

When the institution opened in September 1973, its library collection totaled approximately 200,000 volumes, in a variety of forms. A large percentage consisted of back issues of journals on microfiche; other materials were purchased on microfilm and other microforms. An ample planning budget made possible large purchases of new books before the university opened, including virtually the entire catalogue of every university press in the United States. From a land grant university in the mountain states, the university purchased its duplicate copies of a large number of reference materials.

An areawide book drive was conducted, more in an effort to build good will and interest than in anticipation of valuable works. This brought in approximately 130,000 books; many were of little value to an academic institution, but approximately 40,000 volumes were judged worthy additions to the library collection. A large percentage consisted of novels and literary works, many in multiple copies (596 copies of *Readers Digest Condensed Books!*) but also some valuable titles, including a few rare books. Another university created about the same time had absorbed a science research institute with multiple copies of many science reference titles, which it exchanged for UTPB's surplus copies of novels and titles in the humanities and social sciences.

The first president of UTPB, B. H. Amstead, initiated the practice of contributing books to the library in the name of friends and public figures who died instead of sending flowers to the bereaved. The practice was so well received that other administrators and faculty adopted it, resulting in a considerable number of worthy additions to the library, including many valuable reference works and a few rare books. A staff member of the library would ask the family about the special interests of the deceased and would then select and purchase a book or set of books on that subject. A bookplate would be placed in each volume, dedicating it to the memory of the deceased. The librarian would then write to the family explaining the title or titles purchased and the dedication. Families of the deceased responded positively. Many remarked that whereas flowers were soon wilted and gone, the books would serve future generations of students.

Finances

The upper-level institutions in Texas—initially, five freestanding campuses and five branches of four-year institutions, which were located on community college campuses—were funded by the legislature on a negotiated basis during their first years of operation. Four-year institutions were funded on formulas, based largely on enrollment and student semester credit hours generated.

When the biennial legislative session met in early 1977, the chairman of the Senate Finance Committee informed the upper-level institutions that 1977–1979 appropriations would be on a negotiated basis for the last time, and that the institutions would have two years to prepare for formula funding (an upper-level formula study committee was already engaged in developing the formulas). Just before the session adjourned, due to a shortfall in state funds the lieutenant governor directed the Senate Finance Committee to fund all upper-level institutions on a formula basis effective in the fall of 1977.

The change of funding without time to adjust adversely affected all of the upper-level institutions, but as a small institution UTPB was hit hardest. Through negotiated funding, allowance had been made for basic costs incurred by all institutions, regardless of size. This allowance was recognized, in part, years later in formulas for upper-level institutions. But in 1977 no such allowance was made for small upper-level institutions, and UTPB faced a fiscal crisis.

The final result was a reduction of funds for faculty salaries of 23 percent; funds for instructional administration (deans' offices) were reduced by 40 percent; central administration, 22 percent; and the library, 24 percent. On the other hand, funding for grounds maintenance was increased by 140 percent, since the formula was based on acres to be maintained; the university would have transferred most of these funds to faculty salaries, but state law limited their use to grounds maintenance only. Other physical plant components were reduced only slightly, but under state law at the time the funds could be used only for physical plant purposes. Thus, while physical plant funding was more than ample, the academic function underwent a wrenching retrenchment, which resulted in the elimination of all vacant faculty positions and temporary faculty appointments, as well as large numbers of support staff.

After the faculty committee reviewing the situation had exhausted all of the economies that it could find, it still had to select a few filled faculty positions to eliminate. The review and reductions took place under a severe deadline; the university was required to submit its budget for approval in less than one month. The budget prepared earlier based on anticipated appropriations had to be discarded and replaced by a totally new budget after the faculty committee completed its work.

The retrenchment was devastating to faculty and staff morale, permanently damaging the innovative spirit that permeated the institution and eliminating or curtailing several innovations. However, the dedication to teaching continued for several years, until a successor administration abolished the innovative policy of allowing faculty to choose for themselves whether to be evaluated on research and publication and instituted the traditional policy that all faculty be evaluated on research and publication. This led faculty to focus their attention on research, since, as in most institutions, the reward system no longer placed primacy on teaching. The dedication to teaching that had for several years characterized the institution thus lost some of its luster.

Postscript

As in the case of most institutions founded during the 1960s and 1970s that purported to be innovative, UTPB experienced a mixture of successes, partial successes, and failures in its attempts to be innovative. Mixed results are to be expected when true experimentation is attempted. At one time, UTPB listed twenty-seven innovations that had been introduced. In addition to those cited in this chapter, individual colleges and faculties (departments) instituted other ideas, some of which worked well and others of which did not.

Most of the faculty came to UTPB because of the innovative spirit of the institution, and each brought with him or her something to add to the ideas of the planners. Thanks in part to small classes, but primarily to imaginative faculty, every undergraduate student studying the life sciences participated in field research. Undergraduates in art exhibited in shows that in other colleges would have been limited to graduate students, and undergraduate music students designed and built a harpsichord. Undergraduates in accounting participated in management consulting for small businesses in the area, and history students became the research arm of the Permian Basin Historical Society. In almost every discipline, students had experiences that, though not unique, are rare in large universities.

Many of the original faculty years later revealed that they viewed the early years at UTPB as the most exciting period in their academic careers. This excitement was due in part to the students. At each commencement, when students who were the first members of their family to attend college were asked to stand, almost all of the graduates stood. The students were an appreciative audience. They were unanimous in their applause for the teaching and the competence of the faculty. Most of them remained in West Texas after completing degrees, but some pursued professional and graduate study. The percentages admitted to professional schools were approximately the same as found in other regional institutions in Texas. Given most Texans' low regard for the "oil patch," and the fact that most of the students were first-generation college goers, these percentages alone constituted a signal achievement.

References

Bissinger, H. G. *Friday Night Lights*. Reading, Mass.: Addison-Wesley, 1990.

Boyer, E. L. *College: The Undergraduate Experience in America.* New York: HarperCollins, 1987.

Cardozier, V. R. "Upper Level Colleges Yesterday, Today and Tomorrow." *Educational Record,* 1984, *65* (3), 30–35.

Cardozier, V. R. "The Siting of a New University: The Case of the University of Texas of the Permian Basin." *International Journal for Institutional Management in Higher Education,* 1988, *12* (1), 64–73.

V. RAY CARDOZIER was founding vice president for academic affairs and for eight years the second president of the University of Texas of the Permian Basin, Odessa. He is currently professor and director of the doctoral program in higher education at the University of Texas, Austin.

INDEX

ORDERING INFORMATION

NEW DIRECTIONS FOR HIGHER EDUCATION is a series of paperback books that provides timely information and authoritative advice about major issues and administrative problems confronting every institution. Books in the series are published quarterly in spring, summer, fall, and winter and are available for purchase by subscription and individually.

SUBSCRIPTIONS for 1993 cost $45.00 for individuals (a savings of 20 percent over single-copy prices) and $60.00 for institutions, agencies, and libraries. Please do not send institutional checks for personal subscriptions. Standing orders are accepted.

SINGLE COPIES cost $14.95 when payment accompanies order. (California, New Jersey, New York, and Washington, D.C., residents please include appropriate sales tax.) Billed orders will be charged postage and handling.

DISCOUNTS for quantity orders are available. Please write to the address below for information.

ALL ORDERS must include either the name of an individual or an official purchase order number. Please submit your order as follows:
   Subscriptions: specify series and year subscription is to begin
   Single copies: include individual title code (such as HE1)

MAIL ALL ORDERS TO:
   Jossey-Bass Publishers
   350 Sansome Street
   San Francisco, California 94104

FOR SINGLE-COPY SALES OUTSIDE OF THE UNITED STATES CONTACT:
   Maxwell Macmillan International Publishing Group
   866 Third Avenue
   New York, New York 10022

FOR SUBSCRIPTION SALES OUTSIDE OF THE UNITED STATES, contact any international subscription agency or Jossey-Bass directly.